THE STORY OF AN INDIAN BACKPACKER: SOLO IN SOUTH AMERICA

OBAIDUR RAHAMAN

ISBN-13: 978-1519440679
ISBN-10: 1519440677

To my mother Rahima Rahaman and father Abdur Rahaman

CONTENTS

ACKNOWLEDGEMENTS

I am deeply grateful to everyone who helped me to write this book:

my wife Darina Stamova for being a constant source of inspiration and providing valuable suggestions and criticisms throughout the development of the book, for being my greatest supporter, my muse, my companion,

those who found errors and provided valuable feedbacks on the manuscript, namely Gregorio Iglesias, Dounia Hassani, Nicolás Buenaventura, Ivo Caruso, Dimitar Leksin, Veronika Haaf and Maria Kalimeri,

those who gave advice of various kinds, including Ivo Caruso, Lorenzo Fenech and Elsa Reimann,

friends and colleagues who appreciated my writing and encouraged me to continue, especially Abu Thahir Rahman, Francesco Oteri, Arumay Pal, Mainak Guha Roy, Charles Robert and Anish Mokashi,

Nicolás Buenaventura and Dalia Ibrahim for the beautiful and enticing cover design,

fellow travelers and friends who transformed my journey into a wonderful story, who shared with me the adventures described in this book and in the process left a little piece of them in me, specially Sonia Diaz, Hérica Michelly, Fatima Soto, Angela Soto, Andrea Pulley, Raj Basra, Juan Carlos Rodriguez, Marta Eni, Marie Holm, Milagros Bejarano and Gaby Palomino,

my mom Rahima Rahaman, dad Abdur Rahaman, sisters Rezina Rahaman, Evana Rahaman and Tuhina Rahaman for having trust in me sometimes when they have no idea what the hell I am trying to do,

and the new sunshine in my life, my son Dimitar Rahaman for giving me the greatest motivation to tell a story that is worth listening to.

"I Wandered Lonely as a Cloud."

-William Wordsworth

* * *
The journey
begins...
* * *

WELCOMING THE SETBACKS

"The gates of the plane were closed eight minutes ago".

I felt like I was slapped on the face as the flight attendant said this to me in a matter of fact way in Charles de Gaulle Airport, Paris.

I gasped for air and tried to think over what happened in the last five minutes. I remembered storming into the customer service office in the airport. In the heat of the moment, I forgot all the French that I learned in the last two years. Just plain English came out of my mouth:

"I need to pay for an overweight bag, please, help me!"

I did not have to explain that I was in a hurry. It was clear from my voice and a sense of urgency was written all over my face. The lady at the door, an expert in handling such madly running passengers on a daily basis, took me directly to a counter. I gave a hundred euro bill to pay for the extra weight. I did not care for the money anymore but I resented every second of waiting while the lady behind the counter prepared and printed the bill.

As soon as I was done, I ran to the security check point. I narrowly missed crashing into the trolleys and the people pushing them. I felt irked at the people loitering around like the greatest fools on earth and blocking my way. Luckily, there was no line. I came in like a storm and threw my hand luggage on the belt. An old security man was on duty. As if part of the conspiracy, he followed every step according to the rules, taking his time while doing so:

"Take out your laptop, cameras and other electronic devices."

"(The hell)! Please hurry up, I don't want to miss my flight!" - I pleaded while following his instructions.

I emptied my pockets and took out my belt.

After passing through the security check, I grabbed the handle of my bag in one hand, my sweater and my belt on the other hand and ran. I ran to the departing gate, ignoring the risk that my pants could fall off at any moment. I did not have the time to notice the looks the Frenchmen and Frenchwomen gave me as I sprinted through the luxurious sitting area of Air France. When I finally reached the gate I heard this:

"The gates of the plane were closed eight minutes ago".

Alas! I missed my flight!

I could not believe it. It felt like I was hearing a music in my mind. It was the heart chilling background music in the movie *Titanic*, when the ship was sinking.

> What a setback, at the very beginning of my travel! What shall I do now? Will I lose the huge amount of money I spent to buy the tickets? My residence permit in France is valid for three more days only. Should I count this as a bad sign, give up my idea of travelling to South America and go to India instead?

> People will laugh at me if I go to India after making all the plans for South America and announcing it to everybody. Hmmm...but this is perhaps the first lesson of getting used to uncertainty, something I set out to achieve at the first place. The beginning of a journey to explore the unknown, to face the odd situations and handle the setbacks. It already seems that my journey is going to be an eventful and challenging one.

To my defense, I went to the airport with plenty of time in my hand, as always. But when I reached there I could not believe my eyes. It seemed that every living creature in Paris decided to fly at the same time, on that same day, from that airport. I was very eager to get in the line but a airport staff stopped me because there was *plenty of time* for my flight. Only the passengers with immediate departure times were allowed. I decided to wait a bit since arguing with her was useless. She was visibly stressed and was replying rudely.

By the time I got in the line, I had only about ten minutes to make it to the plane. To make things worse, my luggage turned out to be overweight.

I felt an uneasy sensation in my brain as things started to go wrong one after another. I sensed that somehow I played some role in attracting such circumstances. I made the situations worse than they actually were. When I was told that my luggage was overweight, I took a few minutes to try to reduce the weight by discarding some things. But I changed my mind because it was too difficult to decide which ones to throw away and which ones to keep. Paying for the extra weight seemed easier and quicker. But, at that time, I had no idea that I was obliged to go to the customer service office to pay for the extra weight.

Be it my own fault or not, the fact was that I missed my flight. That was the very first time I missed a flight. As I stood at the departing gate, gaping at the plane that I was supposed to sit in, the attendant told me:

"Please go to the customer service office and they will reschedule your flight"

"Okay, but how about my checked in bag?"

"Your bag has been taken out and it will be reassigned according to your new flight schedule"

I took a few seconds to relax and slowly walked back to the customer service office, afraid that they would charge me for another flight.

At the office, I explained my case stressing on the fact that I was not allowed to get in the line on time and that was the main reason I missed the flight. It was not completely my fault. After some clarifications, the airport staff rebooked my ticket for a flight that same night without charging me anything extra.

It was still morning and instead of spending the whole day at the airport, I decided to visit the lab and spend some time with my lab mates.

It felt strange to be back in the city. Everything was the same. The same Luxembourg park metro station, the same Latin Square, the same Pantheon. I felt like I was a ghost gliding through the throng of office goers and tourists on the busy Parisian streets. It felt like a wrong place to be. I was supposed to go away, far far away. The day before, I said *goodbye* to everybody, thinking that I might or might not see them ever again. It felt strange to enter the same building that I thought I would never see again in my whole life. In my mind, I already closed the *Paris* chapter and stored the memories away, looking forward to a new phase in life. That day, as I walked through the very familiar corridors that I walked almost every day in the last two years, it felt like I was paying a visit after many years.

My decision of going to South America was not very well received by my family or my girlfriend or my post doctorate advisor. Naturally, I was a bit hesitant to show myself in front of my advisor but then I thought it would be fun, since he had a good sense of humor. When I appeared in front of his office door, he chuckled at me and I could clearly read the message from his face:

"Didn't I tell you already? See, this is an unmistakable sign that you are doing a mistake by going on this journey".

But there was a voice inside me that kept telling me something different:

> This is exactly the kind of challenge that I need to face. This is a test for me. I must not fail at this point, not at the very beginning, at least.

I knew that I needed to go on with my plan, mistake or no mistake.

It felt surreal, as I came back from my advisor's office and sat on the chair in front of my desk. It was the same chair and the same desk that I used for the last two years. But unlike those days, there was no rush of the daily work. I had all the time to think, to think about the unknown future in front of me.

For the last two years, I spent my weekdays sitting at that desk. In fact, for the last nine years, I spent all of my weekdays sitting at some desk or other, looking at a computer screen.

One day while I was working on my desk I heard a voice inside me:

> What am I doing? Living a routine life, day after day. Is this all? Isn't there any other meaning of life than working hard, making a career, earning money, spending money, going somewhere on holidays and trying to spend the weekends a little bit differently before the Mondays arrive? I have been doing this for

> the past nine years. Sure, I always thought of myself as adventurous and different from all my friends. Apparently, I always liked doing different things and doing things differently. So far, I was bold enough to take my own decisions about my career and personal life and I never regretted for anything. So why do I feel unhappy now? Why do I feel stuck? Why do I feel bored?

I did not find the answers, but the questions remained with me. They did not leave me. There were many activities to participate and many places to explore in Paris. My weekends were totally occupied and they went by fast. But then came the weekdays and the questions kept coming back.

Sitting at my desk I thought:

> Am I unhappy because I am not free? What is real freedom? Does it even exist? How can I understand freedom? To be free, I need to understand what prevents me to be free?

I pondered this thought carefully.

> I am not free, not quite, not completely. Some powerful primitive forces inside me are responsible for this. I don't take many risks in life because I am afraid of hurting myself, either physically or mentally. I don't express my feelings openly because I am afraid of people's judgments. Although, I have ventured into a few relatively unconventional paths I am still afraid of realizing my full potential. Now, why am I afraid? Are these fears rational or irrational?

Deep in my heart, I always knew that I could achieve

much more in life than what I did. Something always held me back. I ruminated on this matter many times in the past. Few years ago, I came to realize that I had a low self esteem that was responsible for this. Since then, I read many self help books and worked on improving my self esteem.

This brought some positive changes in me but eventually I started disliking the materialistic and goal oriented approach of these books. Setting goals and achieving them did not necessarily make me happy. The nature of the goals were dependant on the moods I was in when I set those goals. But my desires naturally and continuously shifted as time passed. When I achieved those goals, I did not get the same satisfaction that I dreamed of while setting the goals. The goals seemed rather shallow and unworthy of my efforts.

Moreover, I felt a tremendous amount of pressure trying to achieve those goals. Many of those goals were motivated by self judgment. They involved changing myself in certain ways. They were leading me to depression and self loathing.

Then I came across a very different approach to life while exploring Buddhist philosophy. It suggested “accepting yourself the way you are”. To me, that seemed the right path toward achieving happiness and inner peace, which are much more satisfying and meaningful than achieving some superficial goals. But I also realized:

> To be able to accept myself the way I am, first I need to know which way I am. Do I really know myself? What does it mean to know oneself? How can I understand my true nature? To achieve understanding the self, maybe I need to know what prevents me from revealing my true nature.
>
> An answer came to mind:
>
> It is because I am afraid. It has been fear that

> has preventing me to know myself and to be myself. But what am I afraid of? I know it. I am afraid of not being liked by others. I always want to be the *good boy* because I strongly desired acceptance from the society. I am afraid of being socially outcast otherwise. And this desire to be the *good boy* was the reason I did not express myself freely. I was always hiding my true feelings, my true opinions, my true self. I have always been expressing myself according to what I thought other people would like to hear from a *good boy*.
>
> As I kept thinking, it started to make sense:
>
> Because I am not free to express my true feelings and beliefs, naturally I do not have the courage to act on them. This is why I am unable to realize my own self. I am just playing roles, the role of a *good* son, a *good* brother, a *good* student, a *good* friend, a *good* citizen and so on. *Good* according to what other people consider, or rather what I imagine they consider. I am just following the duties of these roles and fooling myself to think that is *my life*.

These thoughts kept working on my conscious and unconscious minds for many months. Finally, they culminated in a clear message:

> To overcome my fears, I need to face them. I need to do what I am afraid of doing.

However, as I kept self investigating, I *discovered* many forms of fear in me. Obviously I needed to go step by step, to address them one at a time.

After analyzing many of my fears, I discerned that most of them were rooted in one fear. The fear of surviving without the assistance of others, specially my family members, relatives and friends. Although, I lived alone in the west for almost a decade and felt quite comfortable at it, I was still emotionally dependent on them. The fear of losing their support perpetually lingered in the depth of my unconscious mind. That hidden fear determined my behaviors, actions and interaction with the outside world.

My mind raced on:

> So what do I do now? I need to do something that will challenge this fear. I need to isolate myself and live without the help of others. But, unless I go in a forest and live there alone, it is impossible to live without the help of others. Clearly, I do not have the courage to live in a forest all by myself. But maybe I can do something less radical and less difficult. Maybe I can try to live without the help of people I know. If I can continuously put myself among complete strangers, maybe I will not have the tendency to please them as much.

There was something I could do that would ensure continuous interaction with strangers.

> I can travel. And I need to travel alone. This is something I have never done before. Whenever I wanted to visit a faraway place, I always pleaded somebody to come along. If I could not find somebody to accompany me, I just abandoned the plan. I have never travelled by myself.

Surely, it was not a new idea for me. Occasionally, I felt the need of travelling by myself. Especially, when I met a solo traveler, I felt the inspiration and need to travel alone. I always wanted to do it but never got the *time*.

I knew:

> I am never going to get the *time* for it, unless I make it happen. I am going to take a break and commit myself for a solo journey. I will travel alone and make sure that I do not make any travel buddies, except for a few days at the most. This way, I will continuously face the difficulties of taking care of myself in unknown places, in unknown situations. There is a feeling of security associated with familiarity, familiarity with the place, familiarity with the people. I need to break that comfort zone and go far away from home, preferably to difficult places with different cultures and languages. I have already lived or travelled in the USA and a few countries in Europe. However, it has been rather easy. This time, I am going to choose a difficult place and travel alone. What about somewhere in Africa?

The idea came easily to me but the difficult part was to even contemplate going there all by myself and finding my way around. I knew nothing about Africa and I knew nobody in Africa. What I knew was that it was a more difficult place than the Western world.

I was contemplating this idea for a couple of months. One day I mentioned this to my Moroccan friend Dounia:

"Dounia, I have a crazy idea, I am thinking of taking a

break in my career and travel around."

"Really? That sounds exciting!"

"I know that it is a very common thing to do for a Westerner but I don't know any of my Indian friends who did this."

"Hmmm...I know it is not very common outside the Western world. Do you know where you want to travel?"

"I have no concrete idea yet, but I was thinking about somewhere in Africa."

"You know what? Last year I went to Peru for a couple of months."

"Really? Peru? Nice! Did you go there for travelling?"

"No, I went there to do an internship. You should go there. I made many friends when I was there. I can help you get in touch with some of them if you want to visit Peru."

Dounia went on telling me many things about her experiences in Peru.

She made me think:

> This seems like a great opportunity. Although I feel the need to travel alone, I simply do not have the courage to do it right away. It is difficult to jump into a solo journey in Africa or South America without knowing anybody. If I can make some connections with the local people, they can help in familiarizing me with the place a little bit. And then I can slowly build up enough confidence to start travelling on my own. Moreover, I always dreamed of seeing Machu Picchu, this seems like a chance to realize that dream.

When I expressed my interest, Dounia gave me the contact of her Peruvian friend, Sonia. After several emails and conversations on Skype, I was assured that she was a reliable person. Over the next few months we became online friends.

I had another Peruvian friend Juancarlos who was my

classmate during doctoral studies in the USA. After finishing his degree and a following postdoctorate, he went back and settled in Peru. When I wrote him about my plan to go to Peru, he invited me to visit his home and meet his family. This made me feel even more confident.

So I started to plan for my trip for the next few months. I shortened the period of my postdoctorate work from three years to two years and made all the plans to take a year off. I did not want to travel for the whole year. I also wanted to stay with my family in India, possibly do some volunteer work and give myself a lot of time to relax, read and think.

Sonia provided all the documents needed for my visa application and invited me to stay in an empty room in her apartment. Everything was going according to the plan, or that's what I thought at that moment.

~ • ~

As I sat ruminating at my desk that day, I felt that something in me was welcoming such setbacks. I was not afraid to put myself in such a comical situation. Missing the flight was not even the first hurdle. About a month ago, I found myself in a similarly helpless situation when I was told:

"With an Indian passport, you can get a tourist visa valid for thirty days."

I was in a shock when I heard this from the lady in the Peruvian consulate in Paris. I was under the impression that everybody was eligible to get the six month long tourist visa. The information on the website was not clear about it.

I already booked my flights and planned to stay in Peru for a few months.

> What would I do now? For the last six months or so I have been dreaming about this trip. I have made all the plans and spent a lot of money to book the tickets. I made many

> contacts in Peru and even started learning Spanish. Will all these be wasted? Going such a long way for a month does not make much sense. I should have called the consulate and asked for the details about the visa before making any plans, at all. I did not apply for any jobs in the meantime. If I cannot go to South America, I will have to go back to India now.

Going back to India was probably not such a bad option, but I could not believe that my dream of going to South America would come to such a disappointing end.

I was frustrated as well as furious:

> This is really unfair to discriminate between the citizens of different countries in this way. I understand that some unscrupulous Indians take wrong advantage of such visas. They enter foreign countries using tourist visas and do not return home. This is surely a problem. But, I have never taken any such advantage. So I should not be the one who should pay the penalty. I had no problems getting a student visa for USA and a work visa for France but I had no clue that this would be the situation for Peru.

I knew that this was a tourist visa and the rules were different for this kind of visa. However, I could not help being jealous of the citizens of the developed countries who had a lot of visa related privileges.

At any other time, I would usually compromise and be satisfied with whatever I got. But this time there was a big dream in question. So I thought I needed to do something. This was a part of my journey, a journey toward overcoming the fear of directly expressing my needs.

At that moment, another Peruvian lady who worked in the consulate, came over to the desk. I tried to explain my case to her:

"I checked on the website. It is written there that I could apply for a tourist visa for six months. So I planned my trip accordingly. Can you please give me a visa for six months?"

"Can you show me your passport please?"

I gave her my passport. She checked it and told me:

"With your passport you are eligible to get a visa for one month."

"But nothing like that is mentioned on the website. I was under the impression that I could get a visa for six months"

"No, the Indian passport holders can get a visa for one month. What are you going to do there for six months?"

"I want to explore the whole country, there are many things to see in Peru. I also have friends in Peru, I plan to stay with them for some time and explore the culture."

"I see, I can try to explain your case to our boss. If he allows, we can extend it a bit longer but I must tell you that he is very strict about these things."

"I will be very grateful if you can do that for me. I have all the documents with me. I can assure you that I am not going to stay there beyond the allowed time period. I am a researcher, I lived in the USA for seven years and I am currently working as a postdoc in CNRS".

"Ok I will see what I can do. Please give me all your documents and I will show them to our boss".

I gave her all the documents and waited patiently, hoping. She came back in ten minutes and told me:

"Okay I showed your documents to the boss. He checked everything and said that you could get a visa for two months but not more than that".

I felt relieved hearing that. Spending two months in Peru would be something significant. But I was not fully satisfied with that:

"Thank you very much. I really appreciate this. But you know, I have made all the plans for a long visit. Is there any way I can get a visa, at least, for three months?"

"The boss said that this is the maximum you can get. It is rather unusual for him to be lenient with the visa. You are lucky that you got two months."

"Yes, I am happy with this but extending it for just another month will really make the best out of my trip".

"As I told you, He is very strict about it. Pushing him again can be risky."

"Ok, I understand."

"You will have to change the date of your return flight before we can accept the application".

My mind was racing on my way back from the consulate.

> Why does it have to be so difficult? I will be in a rush to cover Peru in two months. I won't be able to relax and take things slowly as I initially planned. Can't I extend my visa once I reach Peru?

I did some research on this topic. It was not possible to extend tourist visas in Peru. Since I was not allowed to get a visa at the border, it was also not possible to leave Peru to a neighboring country and reenter with another tourist visa. With my Indian passport none of the tricks and shortcuts used by the Westerners would work.

The whole weekend, I brainstormed for the possibility to get some more travel time but there seemed to be no way out.

So I gave up trying and decided to settle for two months. But at the very last moment I had an idea and I decided to give it a try, just in case. I wrote a long letter containing the full details of my background and an earnest request for the permission of a longer stay. Finally, I submitted the visa application containing all the required documents along with that letter and the photocopies of my degree certificates and resume.

My effort did not go to waste. I was granted a multiple entry visa, valid for three months. My joy was boundless. It gave me flexibility and plenty of time to explore.

The success with the Peruvian visa prompted me to apply for a Brazilian visa. I got a three months multiple entry visa, this time without any trouble.

One week before my flight, I started working for the Bolivian visa application. It required a few days of running around the city doing some paperwork, something I hated doing, especially in Paris. Moreover, I needed to submit my passport for a few days as a requirement for the visa processing. As it was too close to my departure date, I had the risk of not having my passport with me when I needed to fly. So I abandoned the process in the middle.

However, the girl in the consulate told me that I could get a visa on arrival at the border of Bolivia with an Indian passport.

So I thought I would just get the visa at the border to get into Bolivia. I had no idea that some surprise was waiting for me. Nevertheless, I was ready for some adventure.

I got up from the desk and went out for my last lunch in Paris.

IN THE LAND OF THE INCAS

After a long flight I finally arrived in Lima. Sonia received me at the airport. Since the moment I saw her, she took charge of me like a guardian angel. She took me to her nice and big apartment and showed me the extra room. She helped me to buy some necessities, learn some basic Spanish, showed me some places in Lima and introduced me to some of her friends and colleagues. She had an enormous network of friends and relatives spanning over Peru and many other countries in the world. In return of her favors, I cooked some Indian food and taught her Yoga.

To me, Lima looked like any megacities in India, busy, crowded and noisy. It even had a huge population comparable to the populations of big cities in India. Although I did not understand the language very well, I felt at home in Lima except when I saw female bus conductors whom we never see in India. Especially when I heard loud music in the buses and supermarkets, I knew I was in South America. I also noticed that every restaurant I visited had a television set. People loved watching comedy shows on television while eating.

I visited some museums, churches and restaurants in Lima. One day Sonia's best friend Fatima invited us to visit her family in the outskirt of Lima. Later, three of us went on a camping trip in the weekend. Since Fatima did not speak English, I was forced to speak Spanish with her. Although I could only make small talks and silly jokes, this was a very good practice to improve my speaking skills and more importantly to gain some confidence.

Just like Sonia, Fatima was very kind and helpful. She gave me company to visit some places in Lima. She always treated me like an old friend.

Then my friend Juancarlos invited me to attend his nephew's birthday party. This was a great experience of authentic Peruvian culture. I was welcomed there like a close relative. There was delicious homemade Peruvian food and drinks. I especially liked a drink made by boiled corn of purple color. This was a kids party but nothing like the ones I attended in India. The small living room quickly filled up by many young kids accompanied by their parents. It practically turned into a night club with loud music and eager dancers, young and old alike. They hired a young and talented joker who made the best out of the party by involving everybody in the fun. All the kinds were sent home with loads of gifts and candies. I was no exception.

∽ • ∾

Everything was fine in Lima except the wet and cold climate that started to make me sick. After about twenty days, I left Lima for Cuzco. Sonia accompanied me for the trip to Cuzco.

We took a bus to reach Cuzco in about twenty hours. Sonia had a friend in Cuzco who invited us to stay at her place. On our arrival, we were welcomed at the gate by two barking dogs and a kind middle-aged Japanese-Peruvian lady.

Moving from Lima to Cuzco was like a transfer from

the washer to the drier in the laundry room. The combination of cold and humidity in Lima was unbearable for me. On the contrary, Cuzco had a dry and sunny weather which I badly needed. As we started strolling on the streets of Cuzco the next day, the big sun accompanied us from above and stayed with us the whole day, keeping us warm. This was strange and contrary to what I imagined. In India we normally run to the hill stations to escape the heat on the flat lands.

The food in Cuzco was tasty and the people were friendly. After lunch, we went to see the Qorikancha museum which was once the precious and most revered sun temple of the Incas. The temple sadly stood there as a ruin, preserving the stories of its past glory and wealth which was stripped away by the Spanish Conquistadors.

According to the legend, the temple had a giant relic of the sun god, completely made of gold. It used to be worshipped by the priests while shining brightly in the sunlight, inspiring admiration and awe among the beholders. Nothing of that can be seen today except with the eyes of imagination.

There used to be many other less important temples within hundreds of miles surrounding the sun temple. If straight lines are drawn through these surrounding temples, they would all meet at the sun temple, making the impression of sun rays. The Incas constructed 365 of such rays, one for each day of the year.

The Incas worshipped their dead ancestors. They carried the mummies of the dead Incas to major celebrations and festivals. Even today there is a day in the year when they celebrate the dead and it is a popular event in South America.

The Incas also practiced artificial elongation of the skulls, perhaps to demonstrate social status or superior intellect. I saw some samples of elongated skulls in another museum close to the sun temple.

After seeing the museums, we bought the entrance and train tickets for Machu Picchu. There were different prices of the train tickets for foreigners and Peruvians. Sonia paid 20 soles while I paid about 280 soles. So unfair! The only consolation was that I was supposed to ride in a better compartment of the train.

Indians?
I and Sonia are checking out traditional Peruvian clothes in a store in Cuzco.

Another day we took a guided tour to visit Pisac and Ollantaytambo, two Inca settlements near Cuzco.

The Incas designed their important cities to look like some of their sacred animals. As seen from the air, Cuzco looks like a puma, Ollantaytambo looks like a llama and Machu Picchu looks like a condor.

The Pisac ruin was a hilly area with giant terraces or steps designed for agriculture. As I looked from the hilltop down the sacred valley, I felt like I was sitting on the steps of a gigantic amphitheater. With my minds eyes, I could see the Incas, growing corns and potatoes on those gargantuan steps on a long forgotten sunny day.

Agricultural amphitheater
Pisac ruins near Cuzco

"*Fotos*, *fotos*!" - screamed Sonia, jumping like a little girl.

Soon, I got tired of taking her pictures but she never got tired of posing. I never met anybody quite like Sonia who had such an irresistible passion for posing in front of the camera. She changed her poses numerous times in front of the same background as I kept clicking.

On the other side of the valley, I saw hundreds of holes dotted on a very steep cliff that stood like a wall on the sky.

Pointing at those holes, our tour guide said in Spanish:

"Those holes were used to keep the mummies."

"How did they reach there to dig the holes and put the mummies in?" -somebody wondered.

"They used ropes from the top to get down there."

It must have been a dangerous business. If somebody fell down the cliff, instead of burying the mummy, he or she would have been turned into a mummy, soon afterward.

Among those holes, there was a special catacomb where the mummies of the Inca royal family were kept. Some special steps were curved on the cliff to reach that site.

At the top of the hill, there were some stone structures. Our guide told us about some pre Inca sites among those structures. I noticed some excitement among the visitors whenever they heard of any pre-Inca sites. I imagined that since much less is known about the pre-Inca civilizations than the Inca civilization, it must be more exciting for them. I myself knew very little about the pre-Incas at that time.

I could spend the whole day there to soak in the stunning beauty of the sacred valley from the top, be oblivious of time, get lost in imagination. But since our tour guide valued both the time and the place in a completely different manner, he pushed us to move on.

Our next destination was Ollantaytambo. The first look at the site took my breath away. I entered through a narrow gate and saw colossal terraces or steps that went all the way up to a hill.

As we started climbing up the terraces, the guide informed us that from a birds point of view, the terraces look like a llama. Since we stood on them, we could not perceive it. But when he showed us a picture taken from the sky, it was clear that we were climbing up the neck of the llama.

We took a couple of breaks on the way to the top. The guide drew our attention to the next hill. Near the top of that hill, I could see the impression of a face. It was subtle and one would normally miss it from far but when spotted the face was unmistakable. It was the face of the Inca king, curved on the stones of the hill. The solemn form of the face immediately puts fear in the heart.

Near the middle of the same hill, we saw some curving on the rocks where the Incas stored their grains. The grains were preserved using the chilly wind that blew between the hills. It was the Inca version of *fridge*.

We continued climbing and reached the top. Near the top we saw some windows on a stone wall. They all had the symbolic trapezoidal shapes designed by the Incas. They were aligned in a certain way to keep account of the solstices and other important times of the year.

A smart step toward solving the food problem
Giant agricultural terraces at Ollantaytambo

Some colossal red granite rocks also sat at the top. They were cut from a neighboring hill and hauled on a ramp all the way up to the top. It took a lot of human muscle power since the Incas did not have any large domestic animals to do the job. Some massive blocks were abandoned on the ramp which are still resting there today. The locals call them *piedra cansado* which means *tired rocks.*

I was the only English speaking person in the group and the guide did not discern that at the beginning. This was not unusual. Everybody in Peru presumed that I was a Peruvian. Initially I tried to comprehend his speeches in Spanish. But I could not understand most of it. When I told him that I came from India, he was flabbergasted. From that moment onward, he summarized his speeches in English just for me, every time.

The bus journey back to Cuzco was through endless highlands and valleys, wreathed by snow-blanketed hills. Hidden in the mist was a lake, faraway. I was enchanted. I felt like I was in a dream. A melancholic feeling engrossed my mind. I wanted to get off the bus, stroll on that boundless, enormous valley, soak in everything, be a part of it. But the bus did not stop. It raced on with great haste. While the landscape rapidly danced away on my bus window, I surmised that I would come back there, someday. Indeed, I went back there a few days later.

At the time of sun set, the bus stopped at a small village called Chinchero. We got off the bus. Gusts of icy cold winds blew down the narrow, dark cobbled streets. My body heat escaped with the wind at a dangerous speed. It felt painfully cold specially on the face. My warm clothes infallibly failed to give me any protection against the wind chill. I felt like I was wearing nothing.

The houses were made of stones and the inhabitants wore their traditional clothes. It was a real Inca village, frozen in time, hidden in the high hills, away from the modern world.

It was a great relief when we were lead inside one of the houses. A bit of warm sensation came back on my numb face.

It was a workshop for making clothes from animal furs. A girl, who worked there, demonstrated the cloth making process. They domesticated three types of animals, llamas, alpacas and vicuñas to supply the furs. Then they processed the furs into fine fabric and colored them using rocks, flowers, and even insects found in cacti that gave an intense red color.

We got back to Cuzco late in the night and ended the day with a nice soup in a restaurant.

The following day we started our journey to arrive at Aguas Calientes (hot waters), the base town of the much awaited, Machu Picchu. A shared car took us to Ollanta through the outlandishly beautiful valley of river Urubamba.

Next was the train journey. I read about the spectacular views along the rail track and could not wait to board the train. Sonia was not as eager as me.

"You go in the luxury coach, I take the local coach...awwwww..." -She grumbled.

"I don't mind going in the local coach, do you want to exchange the tickets?"

"No, no...don't worry, you enjoy."

"I wouldn't have minded to travel in the same coach with you, but as you know, they did not allow that since I am a foreigner."

"Obaidur!...The local coach is bad, bad smell...I think, I will travel with some animals."

"Come on Sonia, I thought you love animals."

"Awww..."

"I am just kidding Sonia, don't worry, it will be fine. I will meet you when we reach Aguas Calientes."

Thus, we parted and I got in the foreigner's coach.

The coach had the same standard as any European coach. It was spacious, clean and with large windows. They installed windows even on the roof, something I had never seen before. I leaned on the comfortable seat by the window, ready to thoroughly enjoy the journey.

The train started snaking along the stream. It crossed through hills that stood like tall walls reaching the sky. I greedily watched the stream and the wilderness that overflowed from the sides. Long branches of some alien plant arched over the dark water. The green canopy of leaves engulfed the path of the train, creating the coziness of a fairyland.

In two hours, we reached Aguas Calientes. The stream danced along with the train until the very end of that memorable journey.

Sonia told me that her journey was not as bad as she imagined. No animals shared the coach with her, but it was a bit smelly and suffocating in there.

Aguas Calientes was a tiny, expensive and touristy town. Dauntingly steep hills closely surrounded it from all sides. The tips of the hills were hidden in the mist. Machu Picchu was waiting for us behind one of those foggy hills. I did not know which one and did not want to know.

It is possible to arrive at Machu Picchu, see it and return on the same day. But we planned to stay two nights in Aguas Calientes. That gave us one whole day to explore Machu Picchu.

After checking into a hotel, we went for a walk. With the help of Sonia, we found a local market. It would have been impossible to find it without her. It was well hidden among the numerous hotels and restaurants in the town. Some local eateries served Peruvian food in the second floor of the market. The food was so much tastier and cheaper than the burgers and pizzas sold in the fancy restaurants outside.

I was the only tourist among the few locals who ate their meals while gossiping or making small-talks with each other. Although I could be recognized as a tourist from my outfit and the camera hanging from my shoulder, I did not get any curious looks probably because they thought I was a Peruvian.

From the market, we bought some breads, fruits, water and sweets for the visit to Machu Picchu the next day. According to Sonia's suggestion we bought bus tickets to climb up to Machu Picchu instead of hiking.

"Tomorrow, we need walk much and we need much energy" -Sonia kept reminding me.

"Don't worry Sonia, I am bursting with energy and excitement. I just hope that I can get some sleep!"

Finally came the day that I had been waiting for a long time.

We got up early in the morning and took the best seats in the bus. The man who sat next to me with a large camera and tripods, looked like a Peruvian. He could also be from another South American country, I was not certain about that.

"Buenos dias." - he greeted me.

"Buenos dias." - I responded.

Every time somebody mistook me for a South American, I felt some kind of a guilty pleasure.

The bus started zigzagging and climbing up the steep hills from the deep valley cut through by river Urubamba. The hills were covered by dark and dense forest. In about twenty minutes, we reached Machu Picchu.

"Obaidur, you will see, there will be much people, mucha gente in Machu Picchu" - Sonia kept repeating this in the last few days.

This highly raised the level of my expectation. I fantasized the place to be bustling with people, jostling and colliding with each other, like a train station in India.

Although Machu Picchu is visited by about 2500 people every day, they do not arrive at the same time and the site is spanned over a wide valley. So it never gets too crowded at one spot.

We walked to the main gate and to my utter surprise, I could not see the mob.

"Where are all the people? This is not a crowd! Sonia, never tell an Indian that there will be a lot of people, it will always be disappointing...hahaha."

While I was looking for a guide near the entrance, I got a phone call from my Parisian friend Marie.

When I was in Lima, Marie arrived there with a few other people on an organized trip. We wanted to meet in Lima but could not make it because of conflict of schedule.

"Hi Obaidur! This is Marie."

"Oh, Marie! Hi!"

"Are you still in Lima?"

"No, I came to Cuzco and I am in Machu Picchu now!"

"Are you serious? I just arrived in Machu Picchu with my group!"

"Really? What a coincidence! Where are you? I am near the gate but I don't see you here."

"We just got inside. We are following our tour guide. Do you have a guide?"

"Not yet, but I am looking for one."

"You know what? Maybe you can join us. I can ask him if this would be fine."

"Hmmm...well that would be very nice."

"Ok, let me talk to him and I will call you back in a minute."

In a minute, I was invited to join the group. Sonia preferred a Spanish guide, so we split up.

The first glimpse of Machu Picchu overwhelmed me. Although it looked exactly like the pictures and what I often dreamed of, the beauty and the grandeur of the place was awe inspiring.

When I looked at the surrounding of Machu Picchu, I understood why it was so difficult to *discover*. The city is situated at the saddle of two hills, well hidden from outside by several other steep and tall hills, covered with dense and impassable forests. Nature has planned this paradise with a lot of care and perfection.

After the Incas abandoned it, the city was completely forgotten by everybody for several centuries. The Spanish conquistadors robbed and destroyed Cuzco and many other Inca settlements but they could not find Machu Picchu, it remained unknown, untouched.

Later, some explorers and robbers found the city and looted its treasures but the outside world did not know much about it. Nobody lived anywhere near it. All information about the city was lost to the civilized world except some local rumors and legends of ruins hidden in the high hills.

The lost city of the Incas
Machu Picchu

Finally, in early twentieth century, American historian Hiram Bingham was invited to explore the area but he did not know anything about Machu Picchu. He only heard about the stories of the ruins. With the help of a local guide, he started exploring the area. Fortunately, the Peruvian government built a trail nearby in order to facilitate the transportation between the settlements in the area. It was that trail that assisted the discovery of Machu Picchu.

Hiram Bingham finally reached the valley and was stunned by its look. He saw a huge area full of ancient stone structures, houses and terraces covered by wild plants grown over many centuries. His experienced eyes immediately recognized the significance of the ruin. It was not an ordinary settlement. The special importance of the city was evident from its delicate structures carefully constructed by expert Inca architects.

We started exploring the ruins.

The city sustained a relatively large population. Many houses were built to accommodate the civilians. The houses of the priests and princesses were made with special care. The stones were cut and aligned with a sense of symmetry and beauty rather than mathematical accuracy.

Unlike many of the ancient civilizations of the old world, the Incas did not discover the semicircular arch that efficiently distributes the pressure at the tops of doors and windows. Instead, they designed them using a trapezoidal shape with a solid flat stone on the top. Archeologists suggest that the Incas devised special techniques to protect the structures from the damages caused by earth quakes, a common natural disaster in the Inca world.

At the end of the tour, I expressed my gratitude and took leave from Marie and her group. It felt good to be alone. It gave me time to assimilate the gathered impressions and appreciate the site's grandeur.

It was a bright sunny day. I climbed one of the hills and found a shade. I sat under the shade and enjoyed the panoramic view of Machu Picchu while my mind reconstructed a picture of the city bustling with people doing their daily work, on an old forgotten day.

In the late afternoon, I reunited with Sonia. We ate our sandwiches and took a narrow Inca trail to get down to Aguas Calientes.

At the foot of the hill, by the side of the river, we found a small children's park. It appeared like an abandoned park with nobody in sight. We ran in, sat on the swings, hanged on the overhead ladder and jumped on the seesaw. We skipped and we galloped. We giggled and we laughed. The cool shade of the hill, the murmur of the stream, the soft breeze flowing through the canyon wore away all the worries of tomorrow. We played like two little children, cherishing the moments, joyous to be alive.

How many angles are there?
A twelve angle stone as a part of an Inca wall

THE CAPTAIN OF THE SHIP

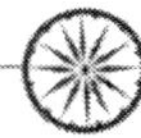

We went back to Cuzco the following day and two days later Sonia left me for Lima. Starting from that moment, I had to take it on my own:

> My real journey begins now. I am going to travel alone, as much as possible. I will meet people on the way and maybe travel with some of them for a few days. But I must avoid having a travel buddy for a longer time. I am going to unknown territories and many pleasant and unpleasant things can happen to me. No matter what happens, I will have to take care of myself. I will have to learn to take care of myself. I will have to learn to be alone. I can do it. I can't wait to start.

Travelling together with Sonia was very useful. I learned a handful of important Spanish words and expressions and basic strategies to survive in Peru. I got an overall idea about how things worked there. I noticed how she approached people for help instead of relying on technology, a strategy that I was more used to when I lived in India, before moving to the West. She also taught me how to be cautious in Peru.

I moved out from Sonia's friends house to a hostel named Hostal Apu Wasi. The hostel provided all the basic necessities for backpackers. The staffs were amiable and helpful.

The hostel was on the side of a hill. From the balcony, I enjoyed the top views of Cuzco. Specially, the glimmering cityscape in the night was spectacular. Although, the night time extravaganza was severely limited by the bone-chilling wind that whizzed over the hill.

In a couple of days I felt quite at home there. For the first time, I found myself among backpackers, many of them travelling alone, just like me. I shared a dorm room with a few other travelers. There, I met an American boy and an Austrian girl, both travelling alone, for a few months. They were much younger than me. Their enthusiasm, courage and independence made deep impression on me.

It was the first time ever that I slept on the upper bunk bed. Every time I stepped on the ladder to go to bed, I felt like I was climbing a tree.

On the third day, I got up early in the morning by a thudding noise.

It was my jacket. The night was freezing cold. I went to bed with an extra blanket but needed my jacket on the top to finally fall asleep. While I was sleeping, it fell from the bunk bed and made the noise as it hit the wooden floor. The previous night my handbag fell in a similar way. Quite annoying!

The two consecutive falls from the high bed made me realize that it would be me who would fall next time.

Coincidentally, the hostel staff requested me to change the room that day and gave me the option to choose my bed. I was delighted to find a bed at the *abajo* (bottom). From Sonia, I learned two important words, *arriba* (up) and *abajo* (bottom). The word *arriba* has the rolling *rr*, typical in Spanish. It is great fun to pronounce the word *arriba*.

~ • ~

Soon I got tired of all the tourist attractions in Cuzco. So, one day, I decided to go on a hike.

The idea of the hike was in my mind since I saw the highland between Cuzco and Ollantaytambo (Ollanta) on my trip to Machu Picchu. The road was about 33 kilometers long. The most beautiful landscape was between Ollanta and the Inca village Chinchero. So I planned to take a bus to get off at Chinchero and walk along the highway toward Ollanta.

The day before, I prepared a lunch for the hike, since there was hardly any habitation on that route. I got some *pan* (bread), *palta* (avocado), canned Peruvian sardines, chocolate coated biscuits and candies made of coca leaves, a good source of instant energy.

On the planned day, I wanted to have a quick breakfast before starting. The hostel provided complimentary breakfast. There were bread, butter, jam, bananas, cereals, milk and coca tea. I took some bread, butter and jam and sat on the table outside to bask in the sunlight while eating.

I met a Dutch couple in their late thirties at the table. We exchanged greetings and introduced ourselves. After the exchange of a few words, I focused on eating instead. But the lady was in a talkative mood.

"So what do you do?" -she asked me.

"Well, I am a researcher. I conduct research in computational chemistry."

"What is it exactly?"

"Well, I work with computational models of molecules. They could be useful in understanding molecular interactions. For instance, computational models of biological molecules can be useful in understanding biological processes and even to discover drugs for curing diseases."

"How does it work?"

"Drug discovery is a long process. But this is how it works. Let's say a new disease breaks out that is caused by some virus (or bacteria). At first, the experimental scientists isolate the virus and study its body structure. They use sophisticated scientific techniques to resolve its structure in atomic details. Then the computational chemists or biologists isolate a part of the structure that plays a vital role in the functioning of the virus and use it as a target. They identify some small molecules that can bind to the structure and disable its function, as predicted by computer simulations. These small molecules are the potential drugs. Then the experimentalists conduct years of clinical trials to assess the effectiveness, toxicities and side effects of these potential drugs. Often all these experiments fail to discover an effective drug but if one drug comes out to be successful at the end, it makes a huge impact."

"Sounds fascinating!"

"Yeah, it is amazing how much you can do with a computer these days. I think computers will be used more and more in the future. You won't have to do experiments using your hands anymore, you will just design the experiments using computers and the machines will carry them out."

"It is fascinating but also scary. So you want to work for a pharmaceutical company?"

"Maybe, I am not sure."

"The pharmaceutical companies are getting very powerful these days. They are money making machines."

"Right, indeed."

"You know, they are trying to stop researches on traditional and alternative medicines. They are lobbying against them so that they can go on selling their own products."

"That's a pity. I do think that there are many valuable things to learn from these old medicinal practices."

"There are many alternative medical treatments in China and India that are getting lost."

"Yeah, in India they still exist, especially in the rural areas. I guess they are also slowly getting lost. As a scientist, I am interested in the science behind them, not the superstitions associated with them."

"I understand."

"And what do you do?"

"I am a spiritual healer. I use techniques like Reiki to probe the flow of energy in the body and use it to heal any dysfunctional parts. Well, you are a scientist, maybe you do not believe in these things."

"No, no. I practice yoga myself and I believe that there is a lot to learn from these things. But I have a scientific perspective on it. For instance, when we talk about energy, I want to know what kind of energy it is and whether it can be measured in a scientific way."

"But you know, when I practice these techniques, I do not need any confirmation or measurements, I can literally feel the energy."

"Right, I am sure there is something there. But I like the approach of science. It tries to remove our personal biases in order to explain nature in an objective way. It does not stop at observing natural phenomena but it tries to understand them."

"Yes, but you can feel these energies and use them to heal without the need of scientific explanation. There is nothing wrong with that, right?"

"I guess that is ok, as long as it does not harm anybody."

"I am not against science but there are many real and valuable things in this world that science just keeps ignoring."

"You have a point there. I also feel that science needs to explore these areas more comprehensively. As I said before, I believe that science can learn a lot from spirituality but I also think spirituality can also learn from science."

"There, I agree with you."

"Great!"

"Thank you very much for sharing your knowledge

and views with us."

"No problem. It was a great pleasure for me. Thank you."

I finished my breakfast, exchanged greetings and got up from the table.

~ • ~

For five soles, a *colectivo* (a big van shared by multiple passengers) picked me up from Cuzco and dropped me at Chinchero.

I started my long walk toward Ollanta by the side of the highway. Soon, the small village Chinchero disappeared and the beautiful highland started to appear.

After walking away from Chinchero, I was the only person on the road. I felt alone and started thinking about the issue of safety. I kept my passport and credit card back in the hostel. Since no lockers were available, I hid them under my mattress. I was carrying my lunch, water, sunglass, cap, camera, ipod, cell phone and one hundred and forty soles. Although I heard that the area was safe, I needed to take some precautions. I did not care about the electronic gadgets but I needed a few soles to pay for the bus ticket back to Cuzco. I took the hundred soles bill, rolled it and slid it inside my sock, hoping that the robber would not find that.

After a while, I got off the highway and took a trail that ran along it. As I walked, wide fields spanned over my vision, white clouds floated across the intense blue sky, a gentle breeze flew over the valley. Occasionally, I saw herds of white sheep and black cows but no llamas. Getting away from the dust and noise of the city was invigorating.

As I strolled on the wavy land, I spotted some black and white birds on the field. Peru is an attractive destination for bird watchers for its large number of native bird species.

Unfortunately, the birds flew away the moment I turned on my camera. The slight noise of switching on the camera was enough to scare them off.

Soon, another bird appeared on the horizon. It was a big and intrepid bird. It was unafraid of any living creatures around it. Instead, it caught the attention of everyone. It was a helicopter. The ear splitting noise of the helicopter broke the serenity of the place until it was gone.

Placid and peaceful
A view of Andean highland on my walk from Chinchero toward Ollantaytambo.

I returned to the highway and took a longer detour on the other side. I was getting bolder.

As I walked, the branches of tall leafy trees arched over the trail from both sides, casting spots of lights and shadows on the ground that shuffled gently with the wind. The warm breeze felt very good on my face and arms.

The trail lead me to a small settlement with about a dozen houses made of earth and stones.

I walked by the shadowy backyards of the houses. Over the fence of a house, I saw a teenager gathering the fallen leaves on the ground into a pile. Two little children, probably his siblings, were trying to assist him. For a moment, I felt pity that they had to do such hard work at that age. But then I saw that they were rather enjoying it. Those children were born and grew up in the nature in its most majestic form. Their little activity was nothing but playing with the mother nature. It was a beautiful sight. Their play with the leaves was more natural and humanlike as compared to the urban youngsters play with the video games.

Timeless
An Andean village

I walked past the village. It was a hot day and I almost ran out of water. I had no chance of buying bottled water anywhere on my route since there were no shops. I continued hiking on the trail that gently went up a hill. On my way, I saw a group of highlanders making earth bricks and laying them on the ground. All of them were covered with mud, from head to toe. I glanced at them from far and continued walking.

Then one of them waved at me.

At first, I hesitated to respond and pretended that I

did not see that. But he continued waving his index finger asking me to come near him. For a moment, I felt offended at that, being signaled without a word or call. But then I realized that probably he did not know how to speak English and he obviously did not know how to approach a passerby in a way that I considered *civilized.*

Working under the sky
The highlanders preparing the ground to build a hut.

I slowly and nervously went to him. Without uttering a word, he vigorously shook my hand with his muddy but dry hand. He mumbled something to the man standing nearby who offered me a mug with some liquid in it. They told me something in a language unfamiliar to me. It was probably the local language Quechua. I only recognized the Spanish word *maiz* (corn) and understood that the drink was made of it. I had heard of the drink before, it was an ancient drink, even the Incas produced and admired it in the old times.

I was pleasantly shocked by this sudden and very

timely invitation:

> How did they know that I was thirsty? Did they somehow read my mind? Hiking in the high hills is probably one of their daily activities and they are aware of the difficulties of going on a long walk in that deserted area. But it was an act of kindness to offer a drink to a complete stranger.

I was deeply touched by the gesture but when I took the old rusty mug in my hand I was horrified:

> Ugh! This mug looks disgusting! It looks like it has been used for devil knows how many years. It is a Peruvian custom that everybody drinks from the same cup. Most likely, it was used by everybody before offered to me. How about diseases? Anyways, there is no way I can refuse this kind offer now. I will have to drink it!

So I thanked them and drank it. It was bitter but refreshing.

The men were busy laying the bricks. An elderly woman sat nearby with a little girl. I gave some biscuits to the girl, feeling grateful for their hospitality and glad that I had something to return the favor.

~ • ~

Recharged and happy, I continued my journey on the trail which lead me up the hill. There was nobody around, the big trees were gone.

When I got to the top, I found myself on a plateau that extended from horizon to horizon. A range of snow topped hills wreathed around it. Near the trail, a little shallow pond reflected the sky and the white clouds floating in it.

The pace of my walk reduced. I stepped off the trail and dawdled toward the pond, as if sleepwalking. I sat by it and looked at the faraway hills, proud with their daunting heights but mysteriously silent. Like an old wise man.

Peruvian panorama
A view from the hilltop

The purity, vigor and richness of the colors hypnotized me. The dark hills, the white clouds, the blue sky, the yellowish green grassland, they all blended into a surreal landscape.

My never ending train of thought processes started losing momentum. I sunk into a dreamlike state. The agonies of the past and the worries of the future faded away. I forgot where I came from and where I was going. I forgot what I was doing and what I was planning to do. I sat there mesmerized by the view, crystallized by the stillness, infiltrated by the eerie silence.

I was glad that I was alone there. I knew what Sonia would have said if she was there: *so beautiful*. This would have ruined it for me. Speechlessness is a prerequisite to appreciate such an experience. Any attempt to describe it spoils it. When we say *so beautiful*, we judge. When we judge, we belittle it. At an overwhelming moment like that, we cannot do anything about our limited ability to perceive, but at least we can do away with our even more limited ability to express.

There was nobody close by me. At a long distance, I saw one or two shepherds with their large stocks of sheep. It was a perfect place and time to meditate. So I sat down in a lotus position by the side of the pond and closed my eyes. But in a couple of minutes I felt that I was losing the rare opportunity to enjoy such a magnificent landscape right in front of me. So I abandoned the idea of meditating and just sat there in silence, enjoying the panoramic view.

Hypnotizing!
The serenity of the place puts you in a trance.

Fully rejuvenated, I continued on the trail and made a

long detour back to the highway. Soon it started to get dark.

Believe it or not, near the end of my walk, I was again invited by another group of farmers for a drink. They were working on the field and building a house using mud. It was a much merrier group than the one I met before, probably because they just finished their work and started to relax, socialize and share drinks and food before heading back to home.

There were men and women, old and young, workers and watchers on the open field, under the clear sky, enjoying the time together, just like their ancestors did hundreds of years ago.

Again, communicating with them was a difficult undertaking. There were a couple of little girls who could understand and speak some English words, probably learned in school. I encouraged them to try to speak in English but it was very difficult for them, specially to make a complete sentence. Nevertheless, they were bursting to demonstrate their linguistic skills that were perceived as superior than their parents or grandparents.

They were all very curious about me and asked me many questions. A muscular man in his thirties asked me, in Spanish:

"Where are you from? Which country?"

"I am from India, Do you know India?"

He did not respond to my question. I could see signs of confusion on his face and thought:

> Is it possible that he has never heard of India? Or perhaps, he simply did not understand me.

At that moment, a younger man standing nearby intervened. He nodded his head up and down with enthusiasm and said:

"Of course, we know India, we hear about it all the time in the television and radio. I heard there are many people in India. Is that true?"

"Yes, there are a lot of people there."

"How far is it?"

"Oh, it is very far. It is on the other side of the world."

He was very impressed by that and the others nodded in appreciation. They kept asking me questions:

"How is the land there?"

"It is similar to here. There are large fields, mountains, rivers etc."

"Why did you come here?"

"I came here to travel."

"How long will you be here?"

"I will be here for a few months."

"A few months!"

They were surprised by that. I clarified:

"I quit my job and took off some time to travel around South America. There is a lot to see here."

"Do you like it here?"

"Yes, very much. I like the beautiful landscape, the culture, the history, the people and specially, the food."

They nodded and smiled.

"Are you married?"

"No, I am not. This is why it is easy for me to travel."

They offered me some jumbo-sized grains of boiled corns. The corns had different colors: purple, white, yellow; not so tasty but very filling. The men were very eager to offer me the drinks.

They were all in a joyous mood and cracked jokes all the time. They had a sense of humor in accordance with their lives: simple and unrefined.

One of the men told me:

"You are not married, right? You should find a Peruvian girl and marry her. There are many beautiful girls here."

"Hahaha...you are right, there are many beautiful girls in Peru."

Another man pointed at an old woman in the group

and told me:

"Look over there, she is single."

The old woman, who sat on a log of wood nearby, came over to join the fun. She was sort of a comedian. She looked at me with a big smile showing the wide gaps left by some missing teeth. The young and the old alike saw the reaction on my face and broke into a hysterical laughter. They laughed like there was no tomorrow, shrieking in delight, thumping foot on the ground, shaking uncontrollably and gasping for air.

Then the old lady asked me if I had something to give her, anything would do. I had some biscuits and coca candies. I distributed them to her and others.

Thus, we spent some simple and joyful moments together on the field, eating, drinking and laughing, as the sun went down. It was time to say goodbye.

They showed me the bus stop nearby. I got in the local bus heading to Cuzco.

The return bus journey was not as nice as the one in the morning. The bus was overcrowded and had a foul smell. It stopped every few minutes to drop off and pick up passengers and created a lot of dust that made me sick. It felt like an endless journey. I was very happy to finally get out of it.

After getting back to the hostel, I took out the hundred soles bill from my sock. Astonishingly, it did not smell like *feet* as I anticipated.

~ • ~

My next destination after *Cuzco* was the city Puerto Maldonado in the Amazon. Taking the overnight bus to Puerto Maldonado turned out to be quite an adventure.

When I reached the bus station, it was dark already. The station was jam packed with people. They looked like moving shadows in the grim yellow light. It seemed that everyone carried all their earthly possessions with them that night. Every single passenger, including the young ladies with high heels, looked like a porter. They carried, lifted, pulled, pushed and dragged around huge suitcases, bags, boxes, sacks and bundles. Many villagers brought loads of vegetables, grains and produce to sell them in Cuzco. As I made my way through, everyone hurried, struggled, sweated, collided, stumbled, screamed and quarreled all around me.

The buses tightly lined up side by side in a long row. The girl at the information desk gave me a stand number when I inquired about my bus. When I reached there, I saw a huge line of people standing in between two buses. They seemed to be waiting for putting their luggage in while the bus driver ate his dinner at the driver's seat.

I hurried to get in the line and waited there for a while. Although, the line did not move at all in half an hour, everybody remained calm and patient. The scheduled departure time passed by, but that did not disturb them either.

Then, I heard a noise. It came from the engine of the bus on the right side. It was on. I presumed that to be my bus but nobody opened the door or checked in the luggage. The people were still standing in the line, unperturbed. In a couple of minutes, the bus started moving back. I got confused. Perhaps, it was making space for loading the luggage. It was a double-decker bus and I booked a ticket for an inclinable seat at the lower level. I saw that the lower level was empty except one passenger. There was no way the bus was leaving! Or was it?

The bus moved back and started to leave. At that moment I realized that the upper level was full and the bus was really leaving. The lower level, which was more expensive, remained unsold except that one passenger and me. While I was waiting in the darkness on the wrong side of the bus, the luggage were checked in from the other side, without me realizing it. Alas!

Before I could decide what to do next, the bus started to gain speed. Earlier that day, I saw a dog chasing a car and thought how silly the dog was. Little did I know that I would be doing the same in the evening. I ran after the bus with my huge backpack. I was so stupefied by the incredibility of the event that I even forgot to shout while running. Anyhow, I did not know the Spanish word for stopping.

I failed to catch up with the bus, gave up running and stood there watching my bus go away, leaving me behind.

> How foolish all this is! I cannot believe it. I cannot believe that happened to me, for real. How stupid. First I miss the flight and now I miss the bus? What on earth is going on? It is true that missing the flight was not completely my fault. But this time it is. I should have asked the people in the line which bus they were waiting for. I have a habit of avoiding any interaction with the strangers around me, especially when I don´t speak the language very well. But this was not the right thing to do here. Anyhow, It feels so strange, almost eerie but thrilling at the same time. Stupid or not, it makes my journey eventful, interesting, even worthwhile. It is exactly the kind of incidence that needs to happen to me and I need to learn from it. I need to be more adequate and proactive. I need to be comfortable interacting with people. This journey is going to be an exciting one. I wonder what is coming next.

A few moments later, I stopped philosophizing and started thinking what to do next. Fortunately, there was another bus operated by a different company but going on the same route. Within an hour, I was on my way to Puerto Maldonado, a city in the Amazon rainforest.

THE JUNGLE BOOK

I did not get much sleep that night except in the early morning. When I got up, I saw the bus running through the rainforest, the Amazon! The home of many exotic and alien creatures like pink dolphins, armadillos, piranhas and anacondas, to name a few.

Puerto Maldonado was like another planet compared to Cuzco. I jumped a season, from freezing cold to scorching hot in about eleven hours. It felt as if I was a frozen meat taken out of the freezer and directly put on the sizzling frying pan. In Cuzco, I heard that it would be *super calor en la selva* (super hot in the forest) but I did not quite realize how hot it could be until I reached there.

I checked into a hostel, next to the main plaza of Puerto Maldonado. The hostel was clean and the caretakers were friendly. It had a small garden at the middle, full of strange looking tropical plants.

The breakfast was included in the rent. I was served with some scrambled eggs, bread, butter, milk and tea on a big table. There I met an undergraduate student of marine biology from California, a graduate student of ornithology from Michigan, another American undergraduate student and a Peruvian girl who studied in the USA.

The student of ornithology had peculiarly large blue eyes and there was a curious ease and gentleness about the way he moved. He was born to be a bird watcher.

They all started talking about sports and other events in America. It reminded me of my life there during graduate studies. I did not feel like talking much. So, I just listened to them while enjoying my breakfast.

The student of ornithology stayed behind while the others finished their breakfast and left the table.

"How long are you going to be here?" - I asked him.

"I came here a month ago and I will stay for another."

"So you are researching on birds in Peru?"

"I am doing a project on some species of birds in the Peruvian Amazon. I come here every year during the summer."

"Nice, I heard that there is a great variety of birds in Peru. Do you also take pictures of the birds that you observe?

"Well, usually I don't take pictures of the common birds but when I see some rare ones I do take pictures."

"You must have a very powerful camera."

"In fact I have a simple digital camera."

"Really? Can you take good pictures with that? I mean, from far? Is the zoom good enough?"

"A few times I took pictures by holding my binocular in front of the lens of the camera. It does not come that bad. You can try it."

"Ah! That's interesting. I have never thought it could work this way. So you spend a lot of time sitting and watching the birds, I guess?"

"Yes, I observe them for a few hours and collect data."

"You need to do this every day?"

"Yes, I am watching a group of birds."

"So what are you exactly interested in, what is the topic of your research?"

"I am studying the cooperative behavior of a group of birds. Here in the Amazon, sometimes birds of different species make a group and search for food together. Considering their different food habits, it is unusual that they work together."

"Very interesting. How long have you been watching this group?"

"I started last year and I am continuing to collect data this year."

"And how do you recognize these birds? Do you see them in the same place, everyday?"

"Well, I have marked some of them. I can recognize them by the bands that I have put on their legs."

"Wow! So you had to catch them?"

"Yeah, I caught some of them last year."

"Hmmm..."

As a computational chemist, my work involved sitting in front of the computer the whole day. For a few years, I even spent my days sitting in an office room that did not have any windows, deprived of natural light and fresh air. I always pined for some field work out in the nature as a part of research. And that guy was doing exactly the same, that also, in one of the most exotic places in the world.

There were two other guys in my dorm room, Raj and Andrea. Raj was an Indian but born and brought up in England. Andrea was from Italy. They met in that hostel and stayed there for quite a few days before I came. They communicated with each other in Spanish. There was a peculiar disparity between the physiques of these two guys. Raj was thin, weak and slightly hunch-backed. Andrea was strong and well built.

Back in Lima, I read about some vaccines,

recommended as precautions against some diseases in the Amazon. Before starting my journey, I took a shot of yellow fever vaccine. I was reluctant to take the Malaria pills. Instead, I bought an insect repellant after arriving in Puerto Maldonado. But I was still wondering about it.

"Is it necessary to take the Malaria pills? I read that they can be harmful to the body." - I asked Raj and Andrea.

"Oh man! I had Malaria a few weeks ago in Bolivia and I am still taking the pills. There are some areas where you need to take them. I asked people here and they said there is no Malaria here. So you might be fine without taking them." - Raj replied.

"I see. I would prefer not to take the pills. So you came from Bolivia? After this place, I want to cross the border to Brazil and then go to Bolivia."

"Yeah, I went to many places in Bolivia. Which places are you planning to go? How much time do you have?"

"I have not made any plans yet but I do have time, maybe even a month."

"Oh then you can see a lot of places."

"So, which places did you see?"

"Let me show you"

Raj pulled out a big map of Bolivia and spread it on the floor. We sat on the floor stooping over the map.

Raj said - "I really love these maps. With a map like this, you can make your plans on the go. I spent a lot of time near Santa Cruz area. There are many small villages that you can visit. They are really beautiful and you can see many small churches made by the missionaries. Some people follow the route taken by Che Guevara. I have been to some of the spots but there is nothing to see as such."

"I see. How about La Paz? I heard it is beautiful."

"Well you should visit it, it is ... nice, it is a big city, but I did not stay there for long."

"Yeah I also liked it but it is not so nice to stay for long. Maybe you will get enough of it in just one day" - Andrea added.

"Why? Is it congested?" - I asked.

"Something like that. You will understand when you see it" - Andrea replied.

"But there are very interesting pre-Inca sites close to La Paz." - Raj said.

"Yes, I liked those sites but there is not much to see there." -Andrea said.

"That is true, you will have to use your imagination a little bit to appreciate them. But do visit those sites. They are very interesting." - Raj said.

"And how about the Amazon area?" - I asked.

"You can go to the national parks near Santa Cruz. You will really like them. And if you are really adventurous you can go to the national park at the north east part of Bolivia but I must warn you, these places are terribly infested by mosquitoes." - Raj showed me the parks on the map.

"Are there camping sites in those parks?" - I asked.

"Yeah, there are camping sites but I recommend you to buy a hammock. They are very cheap and light. You can easily carry a hammock with you. It is much better than carrying the tent and all." - Raj said.

"Huh! A hammock!" - I had no idea that a hammock could replace a tent. "Is it comfortable to sleep on a hammock?" - I asked.

"Yeah, they are comfortable. I had no problem sleeping on the hammock. You can tie it to any two trees and you will be all set. It will keep you above the ground, away from all the insects." - Raj said.

"And how about the mosquitoes?" - I was not convinced yet.

"You can cover yourself with it and fall asleep, no problem." - Raj said.

I still could not imagine myself doing that. So I changed the subject.

"I have a question. I want to enter the north part of Bolivia from Brazil. Is it possible to cross the border there? Also I heard that I can get a visa at the border with an Indian passport. Is that true?" - I asked.

"It is possible to cross the border but I am not sure about the visa issue. I think you should be able to get it there." - Raj said.

"I did not have any problems with visa. Bolivians are very welcoming to tourists. You should be fine." - Andrea added.

"And how is the transportation in the Amazon area? Are there roads or I need to go by the river?" - I asked.

"There are roads but they are not very good." - Raj said.

"You can also take a plane. There are cheap flights in Bolivia. They have some small planes that don't fly very high. They rise a little bit above the ground, fly a little bit and quickly get down to a nearby airport" - said Andrea with a smile, imitating the motion of the plane with the palm of his hand.

Raj also smiled. He smiled a lot, like a happy child.

"So you have been travelling for a long time?" - I asked Raj.

"I have been travelling for a couple of months. But I will have to return soon. Two years ago I came to travel in South America and moved all over it. It took long. Maybe a bit too long." - Raj said.

"How long?" - I asked.

"Oh man! It was about one and half years." - Raj replied.

"Oh wow! Incredible. And what do you do in England?" - I asked.

"Currently I am working with a travel agency. I help to organize and lead groups of European travelers in South America. This time, I finished guiding a group and I have some time to travel by myself before heading back home." - Raj replied.

"Nice! And Andrea? How long have you been travelling?" - I asked.

"A few months. I came to study for a semester in

Buenos Aires. After finishing, I started my road trip through north part of Argentina to Chile and then to Bolivia. The security guards at the border of Bolivia and Peru did not allow my car to go through. So I left the car with a friend in Bolivia and continued my journey. After travelling in Peru, I will have to go back to Bolivia, take my car and drive back to Buenos Aires." - Andrea replied.

"So you drove your car all alone?" - I said.

"Most of the time." - Andrea replied.

"There were no problems on the way? Isn't it risky to drive alone?" - I asked.

"No it was fine. I enjoy driving alone. The highest risk I took was probably when I crossed the Atacama desert in Chile. But I was well prepared. I stocked up my car with a lot of water, extra fuel, tires and spare parts. It was very dry and hot, but I enjoyed it." - Andrea replied.

I was thrilled to hear about their adventures. Both of them were younger than me but they were so courageous. I never met anybody quite like them before.

The city Puerto Maldonado is located at the confluence of two rivers, Rio Madre de Dios and Rio Tambopata. The city is located just outside the Tambopata National Park. The park provides a great opportunity for the visitors to watch hundreds of macaws eating clay on the riverside, giant otters in the river, big tarantulas and voracious piranhas, among many other exotic birds, insects, reptiles, mammals and plants. There is an island in the river called *Isla del mono* or monkey island which is inhabited by many species of monkeys.

As I read and heard about the wildlife in the park I got very excited. But my excitement waned when I found out that it was quite expensive to go on a guided tour and stay in a lodge for a couple of days inside the national park. I did not have the courage to go on my own, I was not even sure if it was allowed.

I compared the prices of the tours organized by my hostel and by a local travel agent. The tours were equally expensive. I started to feel stuck in a city in the Amazon, not being able to see the wildlife that it is most famous for. After exploring some alternative options I found out about a family-run accommodation near the Sandoval lake inside the Tambopata national park. They provide basic accommodation, food and tours in Spanish for affordable prices, for a group of people. Too bad that I was all by myself. Nevertheless, I thought of taking a chance and trying it out.

I tracked down their house in Puerto Maldonado. After knocking at the door and waiting for a minute, the door opened slightly and a suspicious face gazed at me. Soon, I was lead in by a woman through a narrow path into a living room. Her husband Juan joined us soon. I talked to them using my poor Spanish. I did my best to win their sympathy by impressing upon them that I was from the other side of the globe, travelling in the Amazon with my love of wildlife and a limited budget. It is surprising how one's language skills improve when in need.

Although their faces showed compassion, they were reluctant. They told me that at the moment there were no other customers and it was going to cost a lot more for a single person. I tried to convince them by telling them that I would stay for a long time so that it would be worth it for them as well. I added:

"Tengo mucho tiempo pero no mucho dinero" (I have a lot of time but not a lot of money).

The reaction of that on the face of the woman was a classic one. I could clearly read what was going on in her mind, "here is just another one of them, again".

Juan told me that they needed some time to think about it. I revisited them the next day and we agreed on a deal.

I was happy that I was finally going to see the national

park. I was also happy that I was going there alone. I needed to do that. I needed to prove it to myself that I could do it. But at the same time, I was scared. Who knows what was waiting for me there, lurking in the darkness of the Amazon rainforest.

When I told Andrea about my plan, he got excited and showed interest in joining me for a couple of days. I supposed that would be nice to have a companion for a few days. The thought of wondering in the forest all by myself was not very comforting.

I had one more day before leaving for the National park trip. I considered utilizing the time by visiting the zoo in Puerto Maldonado.

It was a long walk to the zoo. The sun was scorching hot and the air was humid. On my way, I cooled off a couple of times by some drinks sold by local women on the roadside. Those were the only things sold on the otherwise deserted streets. The drinks were made by the juice of some Amazonian fruits mixed with a huge amount of water. They were displayed in large and transparent plastic containers. Different fruits gave different colors to the drinks. They attracted the thirsty pedestrians like an oasis in the middle of the desert.

The zoo was rather small and make-believe. It was a tiny collection of animals kept in narrow confinements and poor conditions. Nevertheless, I got to see some animals there that I had never seen before.

I saw a few macaws that looked like giant parrots, but with combinations of red, blue, green and yellow colors. They ceaselessly made croaking noises.

There were a couple of Toucans. Toucan is a kind of bird that possesses an enormous beak, almost as big as its body size. The intense yellow and light blue colors on their faces, feet and beaks looked unnatural.

A small, long tailed, brown monkey was playing out in the open without the confinements of a cage. Three little girls watched it curiously and followed it as it searched for food on the ground.

I saw some black spider monkeys with their long tails that they used like a fifth limb. They were constantly moving on the wired walls of the cage, like giant spiders with five legs.

Anaconda is indisputably one of the most famous animals in the Amazon, yet I was not very impressed by it when I saw one in the zoo. I could only see the face and part of the body as the rest was submerged in water. It remained completely still. The anaconda was rather small, actually not really small but smaller than what I imagined.

The shock and disbelief rather came from a man-monkey interplay at a monkey cage. A grown man in his thirties started playing with a baby monkey. He inserted his fingers through the large holes of the metallic net to pinch the tail or pull the hands or hold the legs of the baby. The mother of the baby came running after it. She used her hands to pull away the fingers of the man to release the baby. He let it go easily but as soon as it was released he caught another part of the baby.

This went on for a while. A bunch of visitors were drawn to the scene. They watched the fun, encouraged him for more and laughed out loud in great excitement. This was the most amusing and entertaining event for them. I was bewildered to see that the baby monkey did not want to escape but rather enjoyed it. It was an adventurous game for him. But the mother desperately tried to protect her baby and did not seem to be very happy about it. She tried to chase the baby away from the wall but it did not comply.

For me, it was awful to watch the monkey business, a big ape harassing a small monkey. They all behaved like monkeys. The resemblance was undeniable.

There was another resemblance waiting for me to discover when I came back to the hostel and looked at my face in the mirror.

Being an Indian, I believed that I could never get a sunburn for real. I always took a great pride among my white western friends for my brown skin which never showed any sign of sunburn after a trip to the beach. They envied me because their white skins always turned red and sore.

But this time, my face got baked by the scorching sun. The brown face turned black. I had a cap on while walking outside but it was not enough to protect my face from all sides. My black face reminded me of the spider monkeys in the zoo. They were completely black except two peculiar circles of light brown color around the eyes. I wore my sunglasses outside. The resemblance was uncanny.

~ • ~

I made plans to stay with the family near the Sandoval lake inside the Tambopata National Park for ten days. Juan, the head of the family, agreed to provide me food, stay in a hut and a few excursions and walks in the forest for a reasonable price. Andrea joined me for the first few days.

I and Andrea packed our backpacks and started our journey.

The port of Puerto Maldonado was just five minutes' walk away from the hostel. We got in a boat to reach the Park via the river. The boat started. We were both very excited and wanted to take some pictures. I took some pictures of Andrea using his camera. When he tried to take pictures of me using my camera, it refused to turn on. I checked the camera. It did not have any batteries. I forgot my batteries in the charger plugged in for recharging in the hostel the previous night.

> Alas! This is a disaster! There will be no stores or any other ways to get batteries in the forest. I was so looking forward to taking pictures of the extraordinary Amazonian wildlife. How could I forget such an important thing? Such a silly mistake!

Luckily we did not go too far and the port was still in sight. I immediately told Andrea about it and he requested the boatman to turn around. The boatman was a kindhearted man. He turned the boat around and got us back to the port. As soon as I got off the boat I started running. I ran to the hostel, got my batteries and charger and returned, all within five minutes. Such a relief!

Carlos, the elder brother and Jimmy, the teenager son of Juan came to receive us at the entrance of the park. They would be our guides for the coming days. We registered our names at the entrance. It was uncommon to stay in the park for ten days. The serviceman at the entrance was surprised:

"Diez dias!" (Ten days!).

He said in astonishment and looked up to my face. I was prepared to give an explanation but he let me go without it.

At that time I had no clue that ten days would turn out to be too much for me.

From the entrance, we walked for an hour and a half inside the forest. It was one of the densest forest I had ever seen. The plants were unfamiliar to me.

Our guide Carlos showed us some curious things on the way. Large ants marched in a line carrying larger pieces of leaves. It looked like a procession with green and yellow banners. They marched, oblivious of our presence, engrossed in the work.

A little bit farther I saw a butterfly of the size of my palm. It had an intense blue color on the outer side of its wings, which can be seen only when it flew but not when it sat on something, a bit inconvenient for taking pictures.

While we were crossing a small, muddy and shallow stream, our hosts caught our attention to a big bird. I got a glimpse of it before it flew away.

My eyes were searching for the strange and bizarre animals of Amazonia that I had heard of since childhood.

I looked down at the dark and murky water from the

little wooden footbridge that crossed the stream. All of a sudden, I saw something stealthily moving in the water.

It was not a fish. It was not a snake.

For a second the animal showed itself. It was a ray with yellowish brown spots on it. I never saw a ray in the wild and I did not know that they could live in such shallow streams. I held my breath to spot other creatures in the water but I had no more luck.

Procession of ants
Leafcutter ants carrying pieces of leaves.

We reached the lodge. It could hardly be called a lodge. It was a small settlement in the middle of the forest with no other habitats nearby.

There were five or six huts. They used a electricity generator for a few hours every evening to meet some basic needs. The dining room was constructed by a wooden roof fixed around the trunk of a big tree like a giant umbrella and a wooden floor at the bottom. There were wooden tables and wooden chairs. The chairs were dug out from tree trunks with solid bottoms instead of four legs.

There were some hammocks hung on the trees not very far from the huts. One could lie down and see a part of the lake from there. Lago Sandoval is an enormous lake with tranquil black water.

After lunch we went for a walk on a trail parallel to the rim of the lake. We did not see many animals except a few capybaras. They are the largest rodents (mice belong to this family of species) in the world. Although the ones we saw were no bigger than rabbits.

In the evening we saw some caimans (they look like crocodiles) in the lake. They were floating in the water with only their eyes visible from the air above. When I turned on my headlamp, the eyes glowed like electric bulbs. A glimpse of those shining alligator eyes can send a chill through your heart.

We were given a hut that was completely made by the wood gathered from the forest. It looked very primitive. There were gaps between the walls and the ceiling as if designed to welcome the animals outside. The wooden floor was lifted above the ground by six inches. Near the door, the broken floor had a hole of the size of my fist, yet another entrance for the animals crawling underneath.

In the night, a giant spider paid a visit to our hut. We both freaked out. I tried to chase it out. Andrea tried to hunt it down with his two feet long machete. The spider hid in the gap between the wall and the ceiling. After trying for a while, we gave up and went to bed.

We got up at five in the morning and hopped on a small boat to cross the Sandoval lake. Floating across the enormous bulk of calm and dark water of the lake was thrilling.

We saw hundreds of palm trees as the other side of

the lake came closer. After crossing the lake, we got into a very narrow canal and left the lake behind. The canal was just broad enough to allow two boats to pass by each other. Soon it ended near a walking trail.

The spider hunt
Andrea looking for our first visitor in the hut.

A group of tourists also came for watching the wildlife. The group was led by the eldest brother of Juan. I and Andrea were guided by the middle brother Carlos who did not seem to be very adequate as a guide. So we tagged along with that group for a while.

As we walked up the trail, we could hear the calls of many birds around us, some quite loud, some not so loud. The powerful calls were made by the macaws. Spotting the birds in that dense forest was not easy. We saw a flock of parrots that sat together on the upper branches of a tall dead tree and made a lot of noise. A hawk was silently sitting at the top branch of a very tall tree, patiently looking for its breakfast. Many flocks of macaws flew over our heads, always announcing their passage with shrill calls.

We spent a couple of hours observing the birds.

On the way back we saw a grey colored sloth sleeping on the top of a tall tree. As the name suggests, sloths are very lazy animals and they move very slowly if they really need to. They rarely come down from the trees and spend most of their lives sleeping.

The sloths are difficult to spot because they camouflage very well with the surroundings and move very little. But the eldest brother of Juan who was an experienced guide spotted the animal. He had a lot of knowledge about the forest and its inhabitants.

On the other hand, our guide Carlos was exactly the opposite. He, although local, did not seem to know the forest very well. While walking, he made too much noise which drove the animals away. When we spotted something by chance or pointed out by the eldest brother or some other guide sharing the same trail with us, Carlos would point his finger at it and blabber something in Spanish that none of us understood. When we heard some bird calling but could not see where it was, Carlos would make some whistles, apparently resembling the calls, hoping to get a response. But every single time the whistle was followed by dead silence. Even I started to feel embarrassed. He was the worst guide anybody could imagine.

Since we did not opt for an expensive organized tour with professional guides, we got stuck with somebody who was useless as a guide. Andrea was getting very impatient with all this nonsense. He preferred to go alone.

As the sun started to be stronger, we crossed the lake and came back to the lodge.

Right before lunch, when I was walking toward our hut, I heard a rustling on the ground. When I looked down to see what made that noise, I was shocked to spot a large brownish black snake crawling on the ground near the hut.

I came to a halt and stood there breathless,

motionless, thunder struck as it quickly disappeared in the bush behind our hut.

Such a big snake, so close to our hut! It took some time to come back to normal breathing. I decided not to tell Andrea about it lest he should get afraid. But I did not know him that well yet. His brave nature came on the surface pretty soon.

After lunch, Carlos disappeared. When we went to Juan to ask the whereabouts of Carlos, he suggested us to go to the lake and wait for Carlos to take us for a boat ride. We gladly took the suggestion.

When we reached the lake, we saw a boat tied to the tree. No other human being was around, except the two of us. Half an hour ago we saw many tourists and boats at that spot. They all seemed to be gone except that one small and old boat.

One boat and two guys desperately looking for some adventure!

We could not wait for Carlos. We preferred to go without him anyways. So we untied the boat and started paddling. We wanted to go to the other end of the lake but in a different direction from the one in the morning. The lake was roughly a *U* shaped oxbow lake. Our lodge was located at the bottom of that *U*. So there were two directions one could go from there.

The calm water of the enormous lake was very soothing for the eyes, But I knew that the water was teeming with piranhas, caimans, snakes and other bizarre animals, hidden from the world above it.

As we paddled away, we appreciated the size of the lake. We crossed the lake on the narrow side, took the boat closer to the land and slowly steered it along the edge. Many known and unknown trees meshed together building a high fence at the water's edge. The inside was dark and invisible.

Not many creatures were visible since it was the hottest time of the day. We saw a bird with pink feet looking for food in the water.

We kept on paddling for about an hour and drew near a shallow, swamp-like part of the lake.

Andrea told me in a low voice:

The forbidden forest?
Dense plantation at the edge of the Sandoval lake.

"You know, that might be a good spot to see the caimans. I heard that they like to lie down in the sunlight."

"You might be right, I can see a dry grassland there."

"Let's go there. But slowly."

"Ok, but let's be careful."

The idea of slowly getting near the caimans was exciting for Andrea but dreadful for me. However, I was also curious.

We got closer but could not see any caimans. Instead we heard some strange noise coming from the forest behind the marshland. They seemed to be the calls of some large animals, many of them.

The sounds reminded me of the calls of pigs but I was not sure. I was also not sure how a Jaguar calls. So, I was in no mood to go nearer.

But Andrea was very eager to see which animals they were.

In the meantime, I got to know Andrea a little better. During his long trip over South America, he wandered in the forests many times all alone. He bought himself a two feet long machete and a large dagger. He used the machete to make his way through the forest and the dagger for his protection and many other purposes. He had a strong and well built body combined with a lot of courage and enthusiasm.

From my past experiences I knew that too much enthusiasm and curiosity can be dangerous. However, I was also interested in having at least a glimpse of those animals.

So, we decided to take the boat closer to the land.

We reached the shore and saw a lot of mud on the ground.

Andrea whispered to me:

"Let's get off the boat and see those animals."

"I am not sure, they could be dangerous."

"Don't worry, I don't think they are dangerous, probably pigs or something like that."

"Are you sure? I think we should watch them from the boat."

We waited for a while but could not see anything.

Andrea was getting impatient. He signaled me that he was going to get off.

I considered joining him but decided to stay behind on the boat.

Andrea got off the boat with the paddle in his hand. I stayed on the boat with the other paddle held tightly by two hands. That was my only protection in case some dangerous animal hopped on the boat to say hello or for a ride or even worse, for lunch.

Andrea struggled his way through the mud, getting farther away from the boat.

I was getting increasingly nervous. I told him:

"Andrea, get back to the boat, it is not a good idea. They can be dangerous."

Andrea looked back at me, nodded, but did not say anything and kept walking toward the source of the calls. I felt helpless. He was not going to listen to me. So, I warned him:

"Andrea, be very careful, don't go very near."

I did not feel good staying behind and unable to help him in case some ferocious animal attacked him. But with the paddle in my hands, I was ready to jump off the boat and run to help him, if needed.

He went a bit farther and told me that he could see a group of cow like animals. He tiptoed toward them, trying to have a closer look. But as he got nearer, they moved further inside the forest and kept calling continuously.

I started to feel uneasy when he went farther away following them. This time not because of the worry about him but because of the worry about myself.

> The boat is right next to the land. What if some animal got on the boat and attacked me? What if a caiman or a jaguar pounced on me or a big snake fell on the boat from the branches of trees above? Andrea would be too far away to help me on time.

As he started to get out of my sight, I could not stay behind any longer. I held the paddle like a weapon and jumped down from the boat on to the mud bellow. I thought that we would fight together against whatever comes on our way, it is much better to stay together than separate.

Moving through the mud was not easy. Andrea saw me following him from behind and told me:

"Be careful, there could be a quicksand. Step on where you can see some plants and avoid stepping on the plain mud."

I did what he told me. Sometimes I took long steps or jumped to walk on wet but solid grounds.

I was about ten steps away from catching up with him. He continued stalking the animals. A few moments later he stopped, looked back at me with a mischievous smile and bobbed his head up and down in amusement. He could clearly see them.

My only chance to see them was to go nearer. So, I took some quick steps and joined him. This produced some noise that made the animals retreat further inside. As they ran away, I caught a glimpse of a black animal. It could be a pig or a tapir, a pig-like Amazonian animal, I was not sure. But that was enough for me, I convinced Andrea to come back.

We took the boat and hurried back. After paddling for about ten or fifteen minutes, we saw a boat coming toward us from the other direction. When it came closer, we saw Carlos and his nephew Jimmy. They came looking for us.

Thankfully they were not very angry at us. When we got back to the lodge, Juan and his eldest brother rebuked us a bit. They mostly addressed Andrea, partly because they suspected that he was the real troublemaker and partly because he understood Spanish much better than me.

It turned out that the boat taken by us belonged to another person. We had to pay him ten soles as a compensation. That was not much. I was just relieved that nothing bad happened in that adventure, that I was not in a jaguar's belly. Later on I came to know that it is very rare to spot a jaguar, one needs to be really lucky (or unlucky) to encounter one.

In the night we again had some visitors in our room, five or six cockroaches. One was fascinated by my soapbox, another one was licking my face cream box and a third one was licking my comb, how disgusting!

After helplessly staring at them for a few minutes we decided neither to kill them nor to drive them away since it would be either a mess or a lot of work. It was better to accept them as guests.

The shared hut
Every living creature was welcome in the hut.

I suggested Andrea: "Tuck in the mosquito net carefully and go to bed. Don't think about the cockroaches. They would be gone in the morning, hopefully!"

~ • ~

The next morning was more exciting than what I could imagine. When I was walking back to my hut after brushing my teeth in the bathroom outside I saw a very little bird on the top branch of a bush like tree full of flowers. It was really small. I had never seen such a small bird before.

I knew that Peru had hummingbirds, the smallest birds in the world. That must be one of them. But I was not completely sure. The little bird looked around for a bit and stretched its beautiful little wings and tails. It was a black bird except a shade of greenish blue on the neck.

When I was trying to infer if that was really a hummingbird or not, it suddenly took a flight. It flew in a strange way. It flipped its wings very fast with a buzzing sound, just like a fly. It gave a dash, hovered at one point for a fraction of a second and sat back on the branch. That was a very strange movement for a bird.

A few seconds later the little bird showed its real magic. It moved around the tree in erratic motions with some intermittent breaks when it hovered at one place. It searched and tasted the nectar of the flowers while in the air the whole time. That was a humming bird indeed.

It was such a beautiful and extraordinary sight!

This encounter was enough to make my day. But there was more to come.

Carlos told us the previous night that he would take us for a boat ride around the lake in the morning. He felt responsible since we were going on errands by ourselves otherwise.

We went around the lake, staying close to the shore, watching the wildlife. Early morning is the best time to see wild animals as they come out to search for food. We saw many species of birds. Some large caimans were floating at the center of the lake.

We saw a *lobo* (otter) that caught a big fish and ate it with loud noise. We followed it with our boat to take closer pictures but it did not like to be disturbed while eating breakfast. Holding the fish in its mouth it swam under the water to go a little farther away from us. The lobo reminded me of *Gollum* in *Lord of the Rings.*

Then we saw a sting ray and some baby caimans in the shallow and clear water. Andrea wanted to see them from close. He lay on his chest at the edge of the boat and tried to sneak up to a baby caiman and catch it. But he did not succeed. I was wondering if the mother caiman was hanging around nearby.

On the way back, we saw a group of reddish brown howler monkeys searching for fruits on the top of a tall tree. Howler monkeys are one of the loudest animals in the world. Their calls can be heard from a few kilometers away. Since I arrived in the lodge, I occasionally heard some aircraft like noise coming from the far side of the lake. I was told that those noises were made by howler monkeys. If they did not tell me that, I would have thought there was an airport close by. I saw howler monkeys in the zoo in Puerto Maldonado and in the wild this time. But both the times they were not in the mood of demonstrating their vocal power.

It started to get very hot as the sun raised higher up. We were very grateful to Carlos this time since he rowed the boat to cover half of the huge lake partly under the hot sun giving us a chance to see many exotic animals.

After lunch I and Andrea went for a walk in the forest. We heard that there was a small river that would take two hours by foot. We wanted to see it but nobody agreed to take us. So we decided to go by ourselves. We did not know the exact trail but we knew the starting point. So we set out to explore it and see if we could reach it.

There were practically no signs or marks on the trails and many of them crisscrossed each other like a net. But Andrea was well prepared. As we continued walking, he drew a map of the trail, marking the branches that joined or crossed it. Once in a while, if we came across something specific like stepping over a waterway or passing through a banana forest, he marked them on the map. He also noted the approximate time taken to walk certain parts of the trail. Sometimes he took pictures of the spots where we took a turn or branched out to a new trail.

After walking for about forty five minutes the trail started to become narrow. It seemed that nobody walked on that trail for months. Overgrown plants on the trail made it difficult to get through. Andrea made his way with the help of the machete and occasionally made cuts on the trunks of some large trees in order to mark the trail.

The trail became thinner and thinner and we could not follow it anymore. It disappeared.

We found ourselves standing on the forest floor dwarfed by tall trees all around us. No sunlight could directly reach the bottom. A bird or perhaps an insect started to make a strange and scary noise. It sounded like the background music of a horror movie. The whole atmosphere became eerie and inauspicious. I could not resist panicking for a moment:

> And this is how my wonderful South American trip comes to a pathetic end. Lost in the Amazon rainforest and starved to death. I should not have come here with this crazy guy. But now it is too late. I have been so irresponsible!

Anyhow, we looked around to find another trail but soon gave up and decided to go back to the trail that took us there and perhaps try another branch instead.

As I hurried back trying to retrace the trail, I felt something like needles poking in my right arm. Hurt and horrified, I looked at my arm and saw a bunch of needle shaped seeds hanging on the hairs of my arm.

The seeds were joined together by some fiber-like substance. Each seed had a hook on one end. I could imagine if a wild animal accidentally brushed its body against these seeds while passing by and one of the seeds got hooked to its hairs, a whole bunch of seeds would be carried along as a consequence. I did not know which tree they came from but what a sneaky and clever way to transport seeds!

I took them off in a hurry which was tricky and painful.

I was impressed by the tracking skills of Andrea since he quickly took us back following the almost invisible trail.

By the time we came back, we gave up on the idea of taking another branch and moving farther. Instead we decided to go back all the way to the lodge.

While walking back, we took a detour since our thirst for adventure was not quenched yet. After walking on it for half an hour the branch took us back to the original trail in a circular path. After that we decided not to wander anymore and just retrace the same trail.

These trails in the forest can be so treacherous.

After walking for a while we realized that it was not the same trail that took us there. We were not very careful on the way back. Somehow we got off our original trail and deviated to another one. In any case, we knew that we must be very close to the lodge by then. So we continued since it was going in the right direction. Suddenly Andrea saw somebody on the trail. It was a human being! After a few steps, I could see a shirtless person sweeping the fallen leaves on the trail. When we went closer we saw that it was Carlos! I was so happy to see him. He showed us the right way and we were back in the lodge within a minute.

In the afternoon, Andrea decided to go back to Puerto Maldonado with a group of tourists that stayed in our lodge for a night. He was eager to continue his journey to

Machu Picchu.

We said goodbye. When I saw him leaving with his backpack following the group, I felt that I had enough of the forest. I wanted to run, pick up my backpack and leave with him. But something held me back and I resisted the impulse. I thought I needed to do that, I needed to take it on my own.

When they left, the whole place became empty except the host family and me.

In the late afternoon I could not see any of the host family members. They were in their huts, probably sleeping or doing household chores.

So I went to lie down on the hammock and relax.

Really? My foot instead of a flower?

A friendly butterfly welcomed me by sitting on my foot.

I got out my kindle to read a book on the Amazon rainforest. But when I turned it on, I saw that the charge was almost completely depleted! I was in a shock. I charged it fully at Puerto Maldonado using the computer in the hostel. Somehow it managed to lose all the charge.

I thought:

> This is spooky! Andrea is gone, the host family is resting and now the kindle is dead. How am I going to spend seven more days here? Clearly this is another test for me. A tough one. Oh, well. Perhaps, it is good that I am forced to be in this situation. I am away from the civilized world and in full exposure to this amazing nature all around me. There is nobody to disturb me here. There is none of those usual distractions. Now, I have a lot of time to give myself. This is what I wanted to do for a long time. Maybe it will open my eyes to something new. I will observe myself, I will observe nature, I will observe myself as a part of nature. Let's see what happens.

So I focused on watching the flora and fauna around me. There were many butterflies and some lizards. In the evening, two large groups of monkeys passed by. One group consisted of little milky brown monkeys and the other group consisted of bigger brownish black monkeys.

A big tree that must have been in the family of palm trees but with a humongous trunk stood beside me with its large branches of leaves hanging over me. The little monkeys high jumped from the branch of another tall tree to one of the large leaves about fifteen feet right above my head.

It was quite a jump for the little monkeys and the baby monkeys were a bit afraid. I was also afraid that one of them would miss it and fall on my face. But I was rather impressed by their performance. They carefully aimed for the leaf, jumped and glided in the air with all their limbs stretched like flying squirrels, fell on the leaf with a thud and immediately grabbed the leaf and climbed up.

More than ten monkeys jumped like that one after another and none of them fell. Falling from such a height would be fatal.

Those little monkeys did not notice my presence very much but the bigger black monkeys did. One of them stopped for a moment and curiously looked at me lying on the hammock. It probably thought, "This big ape seems to be lazy and harmless!".

The following day I decided not to bug the host family for taking me out on excursions because I sensed that they were reluctant to do so. Rather I thought of taking it easy and enjoy the beautiful forest by myself.

I spent the morning on the hammock and then went to eat my lunch. All those days in the forest, they cooked delicious vegetarian food for me. Those were some of the best meals I had in Peru.

In the afternoon, I asked them if I could take the boat and go around the lake by myself. They agreed rather quickly. Juan's fifteen year old son Jimmy was sitting around my hut. I asked him if he wanted to join me for a boat ride. Gladly he agreed as he was getting bored anyways.

We slowly steered the boat across the lake, saw many colorful birds, the sun set and the rise of a thin moon and a few stars. Before it got too dark we turned back. On the way back we stopped paddling in the middle of the lake and took a break. We lay down on the boat and watched the evening sky. Far away from the daily drudgery and petty concerns of life, I could feel the incredible mystery we are all submerged in. I could feel it in the vastness of the sky glowing in the twilight. I could feel it in the depth and darkness of the water underneath. I could feel it in the softness of the gentle breeze. It reached out from everywhere and touched my heart. I felt like a fisherman under the enormous sky, going on an endless journey.

Mirror under the sky
Sunset at Sandoval lake

We came back before night fell. Jimmy told me that he would show me tarantulas in the night.

I got very excited about seeing tarantulas since I never saw them before. After dinner, I took my headlamp and was about to put on my shoes when Jimmy came and told me not to do that. He explained:

"Es muy cerca" (It is very close).

I still wanted to put on my shoes for protection but he insisted that I did not need them. Then Jimmy and Carlos took me to a tree ten feet behind my hut. I was horrified to see two big black tarantulas sticking on the trunk of the tree. They stayed completely still.

I took some quick pictures with a shaky hand trying not to go too close to them. Then with the encouragement of Jimmy and Carlos, I took a closer look. The sight of the terrifying hairy black tarantula sent a shudder of fear or disgust or I don't know exactly what through my body. I moved away from the tree in a haste.

I did not want to have a second look at it
Terrifying tarantula

I regretted seeing them, at all. Those guys were living with such deadly animals all around them. They showed me the tarantulas like people introduce their pet dogs.

When I got back to my hut I saw a bat inside. All kinds of animals were entering my hut. First a spider, then a gang of cockroaches and now, a bat. Wonderful. I did not have to go on excursions to see the wildlife. They were making their appearances right inside my hut, night after night. I wondered what was next. Perhaps a tarantula. What prevented the tarantulas from entering the hut and biting the guests who stayed in it in the past?

That hole in the floor worried me. It was not difficult to imagine that the snake that I saw before crawling next to my hut could enter it through the hole. On the first day of my arrival, I rolled some toilet papers into a ball and stuck it there to block it. But that did not really work. Anyways, it was just for the consolation since I knew that there were numerous other cracks and holes all over the hut.

I still wanted to get some peace of mind and caught the attention of the host family to the crack. Juan, Carlos and Jimmy discussed the matter among themselves in front of my hut while I rested inside. I heard the word *anaconda* and some giggles followed.

Carlos tried to fix it but ended up doing a sloppy job. It was apparent that they did not take the issue seriously. So I just left it on my luck and hoped for the best.

I tucked in the mosquito net with utmost care. By then I knew that the net was there not only to keep away the mosquitoes but also the other nocturnal visitors in the hut. I went to bed trying not to think about the tarantulas.

Early in the morning next day, I took the boat to see the wildlife near the lake, all by myself this time. I started at six o'clock but that was already too late. I covered a small part of the lake for about an hour before the sun became unbearably hot. I decided to start even earlier the next day.

On my way back, I decided that I had enough of the forest trip. I told Juan that I wanted to leave in a couple of days. I told him that, although I promised to stay for ten days, it was difficult for me to stay there alone. He understood me immediately and agreed. It appeared to me that he sort of expected it already.

So I had the rest of that day and the first half of the next day to explore for a total of six days in the forest.

At lunch, Juan suggested me to take the boat and see the watch tower on the other side of the lake. He apologized for not having the time to show me around. But I was rather happy to go by myself. This way I could go wherever I wanted, I could stay as long as I liked, I did not have to hurry at all. Little did I know what was coming for me that evening.

I took my hat, the camera, some water and started. The boat was small and old. It had a crack somewhere and water was slowly leaking in. I had to throw the water out every hour.

Is it a palm tree?
A bizarre plant climbed all the way up a dead palm tree.

I kept paddling along the edge of the lake, observing

the strange looking plants and carefully looking for any birds or animals. I saw a group of sunbathing turtles lined up on a log sticking out from the water at a low angle and a hummingbird sipping nectar from the flowers of a bush hanging over the lake.

Alone on a boat
I was getting bolder

I reached the watch tower, tied my boat to a tree by the side of the lake and climbed up the tower surrounded by tall trees. While going up, one can observe the animals inhabiting the trees at different heights.

The view of the lake from the top was gorgeous. Engrossed and enchanted, I stood there for some time. A small group of French tourists also climbed up the tower. We exchanged greetings and introduced ourselves. A girl in the group raised her eyebrows when she heard that I was venturing on the lake all alone. It made me feel proud of myself.

After wishing them a pleasant afternoon, I got down

the tower and continued paddling the boat around the lake. Soon it started to get dark. I saw the sun set from the boat.

It was time to return.

Since I was on the opposite side of the lake, farthest from the lodge, I decided to pass through the center of the lake. By then I was quite tired of paddling. So, I moved very slowly. I paddled two or three vigorous strokes on both sides of the boat giving it a momentum and let it drift until it came to a complete stop before I paddled again. This way I could take rest intermittently and it was a pleasant change from the continuous paddling which was wearing me out.

While I was enjoying myself, I did not notice that something strange was happening in the sky. It was changing rapidly. Within a few minutes the sky was engulfed by immense black clouds casting shadows on the dark water of the lake, making it darker.

A strong wind started to blow from the other side. This was alarming. I was still far from the center of the lake and paddling against the wind was getting increasingly difficult. It was also getting strenuous to keep the direction of the boat fixed. A couple of times the wind turned the boat sideways, scaring the wit out of me. I straightened it by paddling fiercely and kept going.

I saw a lightning faraway. It looked like a storm was coming. I was getting near the center of the humongous lake. That was frightening since the lake was way too big for me to swim across. If the wind turned into a storm and flipped the boat, I would have had no chance of surviving in the center of the lake, that too in the blinding darkness, vulnerable to the attacks of deadly caimans and piranhas.

Within five to ten minutes all the other boats on the lake disappeared. They knew that the storm was coming. So, I was all alone in that mysterious lake, tirelessly paddling to go back.

But go back where?

It struck me like a thunder: if the darkness took over, there would be no way to figure out the direction to the lodge.

On the edge of the lake where the lodge was hidden behind the trees, I could see a little clearing in the forest. A coconut tree was standing alone on one side and another tree that we used to tie the boat to was standing on the other side. That was all of the *dock* that could be seen from the middle of the lake.

I could see it but it seemed very far away.

I thought:

> I must reach there before I lose the sight of it. In case I lose it and reach a different spot, I would not dare to leave the boat and get in the forest in the night. I don't have my flash light with me. It would be madness to try to find my way through the blinding darkness of the forest. So, I will have to spend the night in the boat or keep rowing along the edge of the lake trying to find the dock. But There is still some sunlight, some hope. I must hurry up.

I kept on paddling with all my might. A few strong strokes on the left, a few strong strokes on the right, and repeat. I could not afford getting exhausted. I kept my eyes fixed on the coconut tree not to lose it.

Then a strange and disconcerting feeling appeared in my heart. I suspected that the boat was not moving at all. It seemed that I was struggling against the wind to keep my boat at the same spot without gaining any distance. With time, the suspicion got stronger and it started to weigh heavy upon me, it started to demoralize me. In order to overcome the terrible thought, I kept telling myself that I must reach the shore before it got completely dark or I might not be able to reach it at all.

I was paddling as fast as I could, almost violently. I hoped that the paddle would not break or slip away from my hands. That would be fatal. I also hoped that the old boat could make it till the end.

As I moved away from the center and got closer to the shore without losing the sight of the coconut tree, my heart filled up with a sense of triumph replacing the overwhelming fear that captured it before.

When I got even closer to the shore, I felt confident that I could swim the rest of it if the boat failed at that point. That was a comforting feeling; although the idea of swimming with the caimans was not.

Then again, the boat got stuck. The wind was ever stronger. I paddled with full strength but felt that something powerful was preventing it from moving. A terrible idea flashed through my mind:

> Is it just the wind or a caiman is holding the boat? Or is it some superior power that is trying to teach me a lesson?

That fear, although irrational, could get me killed. I fought against that thought, lifted my will power and kept on paddling, steadily, strongly and tirelessly. The wind dropped a little and the boat moved again.

I made it to the shore, finally. It felt so good to put my feet on the solid ground. It was pitch dark on the forest floor since the starlight could not penetrate the dense canopy above. Unfortunately I had no flash light or phone with me. So, I put my camera in the display mode and used the light to find my way back to the lodge.

Nobody seemed to be concerned about me back in the lodge, they forgot that I went on a boat trip.

I got under the shower and enjoyed the water flowing down my face and body. Water can be so refreshing but also intimidating at times.

See you later alligator
One of the black caimans in the Sandoval lake. They can grow up to 5 meters in length.

THE TOURIST BECOMES A CELEBRITY

After coming back from the Tambopata National Park, I checked into a hotel. I enjoyed staying in the big, clean and comfortable hotel room after living in a hut among deadly animals for six days.

Two days later, I headed north to the border of Brazil. I planned to stay at the little village called Iñapari. There was nothing much other than a couple of shops, restaurants, small hotels and a bank.

The next morning I checked out from the hotel and got an exit stamp on my passport. Then I crossed a river via a bridge that connected Peru and Brazil. I was expecting tight security at the border but there was no security at all. Anybody could cross the border without being asked to show any documents. The road was completely deserted except a few pedestrians. The hot sun was shining fiercely on my head and my backpack felt heavier as the road started to climb up.

In about ten minutes I walked up to a checking post

and got the entry stamp for Brazil. The Brazilian village Assis Brasil looked very deserted as well.

The Brazilians looked very different from the Peruvians. They were tall, well built, slim and there was a variety of different races and mixtures between the races.

I could not understand what they said in Portuguese, except a few words. Portuguese has many common words with Spanish but the way they pronounced them made it difficult for me to understand. They did not seem to understand my Spanish very well either.

It was a very small village far from any big Brazilian city.

Before crossing the border I changed my remaining Soles in Peru to forty Brazilian Reals. I used my international debit card to withdraw money in local currency from the ATMs in Peru without any problems. So I was hopeful that it would also work in Brazil.

Realizing that forty Reals was not much, I went inside Banco do Brasil to withdraw money from the ATM. But to my utter surprise and shock, the ATM refused to recognize my card. I tried a few times without any success. That was a moment of panic since I had no money except forty Reals.

I asked a staff in the bank for help. He told me that there were two other banks in the village that I could try. I rushed to those other smaller banks located in different parts of the village. The first one did not have an ATM, the other one only accepted the cards issued by that bank.

All that running around under the scorching sun with my heavy backpack made me tired and worried:

> I am stuck in this remote village without internet connection or any other means of communication. I cannot make an international call with my simple Peruvian phone (I was using internet cafés to do that). With the forty Reals, I can go to a big city further inside Brazil but it would be risky

> since I am not sure if my card is valid in Brazil at all. I should probably go back to Peru.

While I was contemplating on going back, something inside me started to talk to me:

> It cannot be so difficult. I must be mistaken. There must be a way. It is the heat and exhaustion that got hold of me. This is just another test for me. Don't be silly. Don't give up.

I calmed down a bit and decided to try the Banco do Brasil again. I went in and explained my situation in Spanish to the same staff, as clearly as I could.

He understood the urgency of my situation. This time he took me to the ATM and helped me go through each step, carefully. It turned out that after inserting the card I was not pulling it out fast enough to enable the machine to detect it.

When I pulled it fast, it recognized my card. I requested a large sum. A few seconds later, my hand was holding some new Brazilian bills ornamented by colorful pictures of Amazonian animals. It was unbelievable!

I never enjoyed withdrawing money from an ATM as much as I did that day. At the same time it made me think:

> So far, I preferred not to carry too much cash with me for safety reasons. Although it is a good idea, I should be a little more careful next time. I must always carry enough cash with me and withdraw money well in advance before I run out of it. It is not wise to blindly rely on the ATMs and credit cards. Another lesson learned.

The incident also arose a question in me:

It is silly the way I panicked. Was it necessary? Deep inside, I knew that it could not be such a big problem. Then why did my mind trick me into a panic attack?

~ • ~

I shared a cab to go to Brasiléia, a Brazilian town at the border with Bolivia. The drive was through wavy green landscape on a road with lots of potholes. Herds of cows peacefully grazed on the grass. Their white skins stood out against the vast dark-green grasslands, not quite the Amazonian forest I imagined.

I was surprised to see farmlands, one after another. Lots of trees must have been destroyed to clear the grounds for them.

I was disappointed by Brasiléia. It was very small, there was nothing interesting to see and it was difficult to find a hotel. To make things worse, everything was very expensive. It did not make much sense to stay there. So I decided to enter Bolivia.

I had to go to a neighboring town called Epitaciolândia to get the exit stamp. Then I crossed a small bridge and got into a cramped little immigration office inside Bolivia.

The staffs in the office did not seem to have ever met an Indian before. They had contradictory opinions about whether I was eligible to get a visa on arrival. They checked the info in an old computer full of dust and discussed the matter among themselves. Still undecided, they asked me to wait outside the office while they waited for their boss to take over the matter.

Finally the boss came over and told me:

"I am sorry but we cannot give you a visa from this office."

"But I checked on the internet that Indian passport holders are eligible to get a visa on arrival at the border."

"That is true but we don't have the permission to issue such visas from this office."

"I had no way to know that. There was no information available on the website. What do you suggest me to do now?"

"There is a Bolivian consulate in Brasiléia. You can submit a visa application there. When you get the visa I can let you in."

"But that is going to be time consuming. Shall I go to another entry point like Guajara-Mirim and try to enter from there? Maybe they have the visa on arrival facility there. Do you know if they have it?"

"I don't know if they have it there. They might tell you the same thing. Why don't you just go to the consulate instead of travelling so long? It is quite far from here."

"Okay, I will have to think about this", I said with a sigh. "So shall I just go back and reenter Brazil?"

"Yes, if you go back to the Policia Federal they should be able to give you a reentry stamp."

I left the office, got the reentry stamp and got back in Brazil. I had to think fast:

> Yet another dilemma. I can either retrace my journey to Peru or go to Guajara-Mirim and try my luck there. I don't feel like retracing. On the other hand, going to Guajara-Mirim would be expensive, time consuming, uncertain and stressful. That way, I would be going farther away from Peru and it would be very disheartening if I have to come back all the way. My third option is to apply through the consulate, meaning more paperwork and waiting. I hate paperwork and I hate waiting. But maybe I will find some nice place to visit while I wait.

After thinking for a bit I chose the third option.

Fortunately, I anticipated such a hold up. So I carried some useful documents with me. When I went to the consulate, they gave me a list of required documents. I had all of them with me but additionally I needed to get a police verification certificate from the Brazilian government.

It did not make any sense to me since I was in Brazil for just a couple of days. But they refused to process my visa application without it. When I went to get the certificate from the Policia Federal, they took my application and told me to come back in ten days.

Ten days! I was in distress. It was unbearable to imagine being stuck in a small make-believe bordering town with dusty roads and ugly houses for ten days. I could not find a decent hotel. There seemed to be no hostels at all. On top of that I found out that the town or any other cities nearby were very expensive. It appeared that no tourists ever visited that part of Brazil.

After spending a sleepless night fighting with mosquitoes in a disgusting hotel room, I decided to move to a little village called Xapuri and wait there for ten days.

Xapuri was a pretty village stretched out on the sides of a main road running alongside a small river. Large trees cut in the shape of cubes decorated one side of the main road. It gave it a serene and cozy look.

I found a nice and clean room in a *pousada* (guesthouse) for a reasonable price. I spent most of my time reading and enjoying the air conditioning in the room as it was very hot to go outside during the day. The food was different from Peruvian food and they gave large portions. I tasted the fish from the river.

The owner of the pousada, a big fat man, was very kind to me. He told me that he never met an Indian before. Further conversations with him was hindered by my complete lack of knowledge in Portuguese. Only local tourists and visitors stayed in the pousada and nobody spoke or understood English at all.

I picked up a few Portuguese words in the meantime.

The first thing I learned was *bom dia* (good day) which was pronounced like *bonjïa.* I noticed that they often pronounced *d* as *j* and *t* as *ch.* For instance, *boa noite* (good night) was pronounced as *boa noiche.* It was very important to pronounce the words correctly to be understood.

The inhabitants of the small village were very social and they enjoyed exchanging greetings. If you go for a walk on the main road you cannot avoid seeing the same faces every day.

The wife of the owner was a mother figure for me during my stay. She understood my difficulty due to the lack of knowledge in Portuguese. She patiently figured out what I needed from my limited Spanish vocabulary and plenty of hand waving. For instance, she helped me to find drinking water and showed me how to use the laundry facilities.

There was a rich buffet breakfast (breakfast is called *café de manha* in Brazil) included in the rent. During breakfast one morning, the owner introduced me to Hérica, a short lady in her mid thirties with curly black hair. She was staying in the same pousada.

She got curious when she heard that I was from India. She too never met an Indian before and wanted to have a conversation with me. But it was almost impossible to understand each other. She did not know English at all and I did not know Portuguese. She understood Spanish but could not speak it. So I kept using my overused, embarrassingly short list of Spanish words while she replied in Portuguese, which I could hardly understand.

In any case, she had to go somewhere in a hurry but she wanted to invite me to have lunch together. It took a couple of minutes for her to convey that message to me and make sure that I understood it correctly. But she was very kind and patient throughout the painstaking process.

I was not sure what kind of conversation would be

possible with such an extraordinary mismatch of linguistic skills. But I went anyways in order to respect the invitation.

We went to the one and only small restaurant on the other side of the road from the pousada. She asked me what I wanted to eat, carefully listened to what I said and ordered the food for me as well as herself.

We managed to have a very basic conversation. I got to know that she was a high school teacher in Rio Branco, a city close by. Sometimes in the weekends she visited the schools in the neighboring towns. That weekend she came to give a talk in Xapuri.

I was surprised by Hérica's lifestyle. Although she lived in the Amazon, she possessed a SUV, a smart phone, owned two apartments and a house in Rio Branco and had a job that paid well. Pretty soon we figured out that our personal preferences were quite contrary to each other. I did not like big cars and smart phones while she had both of them. She liked eating meat and her favorite drink was coca cola. I preferred vegetarian food and avoided soft drinks. I liked walking while she hated it. She was very religious and I was almost an anti religious person. In spite of all the differences, we went along fine. There was no scope of any arguments due to the severely incapacitated state of verbal communication.

In the afternoon, we went on a drive in her SUV. Hérica felt very hot and wanted to find a *sorveteria* (an ice cream place). We found one three blocks away.

I tried an ice cream made of a Brazilian berry like fruit called *acai* which has a deep purple color and a specific taste. Have a Brazilian as a company was beneficial since I was afraid of trying unknown local food.

Then we went to see the Casa de Chico Mendes, the house of Chico Mendes, who protested against the environmental exploitation in the Amazon. He was shot dead in that house by his enemies. The house which was kept as it was at the time of the murder, preserved the sad memories of the event. Today Chico Mendes is well remembered and honored in all of the Brazilian state of Acre.

The best way to chill in the Amazon
I must thank Hérica for the idea

Hérica invited me to visit Rio Branco when she left in the evening. She told me that she would try to find a hotel with a reasonable price if I wanted to come.

In a couple of days Hérica wrote me that she found a hotel close to her apartment and invited me to come if I felt like. I stayed six days in Xapuri by then and was getting bored of it. So I was strongly attracted by the idea. But I had to think a little bit before accepting her invitation:

> I don't really know her. I read about many dangers in Brazil, maybe she belongs to a gang of scammers or kidnappers. Also, it is so difficult to communicate with her. How am I

> going to manage everything? Hmmm...On the other hand, she is being so kind and nice. I know, I know, the con artists are always very nice and friendly. But my gut feeling is telling me that she is genuine. Maybe I should take a risk and go. I stayed in Xapuri for too long. I need to move on.

I took a bus early next morning and headed toward Rio Branco (white river), a big city situated on the bank of river Acre.

~ • ~

In the bus, a man in his thirties asked me in plain English:

"Are you a tourist? Where are you from?"

"Yes, I am a tourist, I am from India. And you? Where are you from?"

"I am originally from Sri Lanka but I live here now."

"Oh, interesting! What brings you to Brazil? Do you work here?"

"Yes, I have business." He pronounced the word *business* in a funny way, like a snake making hissing noise.

"What kind of business?"

"I sell mobile phones and other electronic stuffs. And you? What do you do?"

"Aaa...I am a researcher but I am taking a gap year and travelling around a bit now."

"So you want to go back to India for work?"

"I am not sure, there are some good opportunities there but I did not decide anything yet. I have time to think about it."

"Yes, there are good opportunities in India. But for business, I think Brazil is a better place. If you want to do business, you should come to Brazil."

"Well, I study science and I have never thought about

doing any business."

The man explained to me about his business in some details. But I was more curious about his life story than the details of his business. I asked him:

"So how did you come to Brazil?"

"It is a long story. When I was living in Sri Lanka there was a lot of problems. Have you heard of LTTE?"

"Yes, the militant group of Tamil Tigers. I heard that the group is dissolved recently."

"Yes, now there is no problem."

"So tourists are coming to Sri Lanka now?"

"Yes, yes, there are a lot of tourists now. I also visited my family last year. But when I was fifteen years old, I had to leave Sri Lanka. I went to South East Asia. I lived there for a while. But after some time I got into trouble. They sent me to jail."

"It was because you were an illegal immigrant?"

"Yes, but then they let me go. From there I went to the middle east and finally came to Brazil. Here I got into trouble again. I went to jail."

"Wow! How long did you stay in the jail?"

"About a month but then they gave me a refugee status and let me go. I have been living in Brazil since then."

"With the refugee status?"

"No, no, recently I got a Brazilian passport."

"Oh good! And you have a family here in Acre? Are you married?"

"No. I was married to a Brazilian girl but we got divorced. I am single now."

"I see. So you speak Portuguese?"

"Yes, I have lived here for a long time and learned Portuguese. It is important for the business."

He loved the word *business*.

As the bus moved on, I looked out from the window and pondered over his lonely life, so far away from home. It must have been very hard for him to be uprooted from home and casted off to several foreign countries with completely different cultures, languages and life styles.

When the bus halted at a store for a short break, the Sri Lankan guy bought me something for breakfast before I could figure out how to ask for food using the couple of Portuguese words that I learned. I felt very grateful to him for his kind offer. I thanked him and accepted it. Although our stories were very different from each other, a bond of empathy and kinship was instinctively formed between us.

~ • ~

I was received at the bus stop by Hérica. She took me to the hotel, made sure of everything and went to her work.

The manager of the small hotel Republica Brasileirinho was very friendly, attentive and he always had a smile on his face. In addition to the hotel, he managed a restaurant. A buffet lunch in the restaurant was included in the rent.

I met some medical science students who were living in that hotel since it was more expensive to live in a decent apartment in Rio Branco. I was very impressed by them as they were bright and knowledgeable. I enjoyed talking to them. It was a relief to be able to speak English and be completely understood without any problems. They were proficient in all aspects of English except the speaking skills, I guess mostly due to lack of practice.

There was a fridge in the common area of our floor. The hotel manager filled it up with fruits and the leftover restaurant food for us. We talked for hours about science, philosophy and Brazilian current affairs while feasting on the food. After a long time I had an intellectual conversation with somebody other than myself.

After work, Hérica took me for a ride around the city Rio Branco. It was nothing like what I imagined a city inside the Amazon would be. The city had a very modern look. It was beautifully designed with parks, canals and biking trails. We visited a library, a church and a palace. The riverside was charming in the evening.

On Saturday, Hérica took me for a visit to her work place, high school Fundação Bradesco. The school was well equipped and very modern. It had large play grounds, computer room, canteen and high-tech infrastructure in the classroom including touch screen projection on the white boards. Everything looked new and clean. Among the students, there were more girls than boys. The same was true for the teachers.

It was a *student activity day* at the school. With the guidance of the teachers, the students prepared banners and posters campaigning for issues like legalization of Marijuana, gay marriage, violence against women, AIDS, environmental issues etc.

English was taught as the second language in the school but the students were not confident speaking it. A couple of courageous ones exchanged one or two sentences with me when I asked them about the posters. From that, I had the impression that their views on several of the issues were rather conservative. In any case, the subject that they were most excited about was rock music. Rock stars were their idols. They put up big posters of Raul Seixas, the father of Brazilian rock music.

Hérica told me that she would introduce me to one of her colleagues who spoke English and who even went to India. A few minutes later I met a tall girl with a long skirt and a beautiful smile. She excitedly talked to me in clear English:

"So, you are from India?"

"Yes. Hérica told me that you visited India. Is that right?"

"Yes, I actually lived in India."

"Really? For how long?"

"About two years."

"Wow! What did you do there?"

"I took some yoga classes. I lived in the ashram. I also took some cooking classes."

"Interesting. You know, you look just like an Indian. When you were in India, did they recognize you as a foreigner or they thought you were an Indian?"

"You are right. Often they thought I was an Indian..."

"But when you spoke, they could tell that you were not, right?" - I interrupted.

"Oh, I learned some Hindi. It was very useful. Like on the street, I would ask the rickshaw pullers *kitna hai*? (how much?). He would say something like *bees rupiya* (twenty rupees) and I would bargain with him, *bohot jyda hai* (it is too much)."

We both laughed out. She had an excellent Hindi accent.

"So where did you live in India?" -I asked her.

"I lived in mostly Varanasi and Puna. But I visited many other cities."

"Nice."

"I had an Indian boyfriend."

"Oh, really?"

"Yes, he was a doctor. I met him in Puna. Then I moved with him to South Africa. I lived there with him for two years."

"How did you meet him?"

"I met him at the Osho's ashram."

"So he is a follower of Osho?"

"Yes. He read a book by him when he was on a flight and that book completely changed his life. It was like he found the mantra for his life."

"Very interesting. I don't know much about Osho and his philosophies but I do like meditation. I plan to take a ten day long Vipassana course. Have you heard of it?"

"Oh yes, I have taken that course."

"Really? How was it? Was it difficult to follow the strict rules and regulations."

"No. It was wonderful. Don't worry. The first two or three days will be difficult but then your mind will become quiet and peaceful and you will be absorbed in the meditation."

"Sounds wonderful indeed."

"So how long are you going to be here?"

"Just a couple more days."

"Oh, you know what? We should cook Indian food."

"Yeah, maybe. But I don't have the spices."

"Don't worry. I have all the Indian spices, *jeera*, *haldi*, everything!"

"Fantastic! So you like Indian food?"

"I love it."

We said goodbye for the moment because she had to assist in organizing the event.

Then Hérica introduced me to Marta, the director of the high school, an energetic, amiable and cheerful lady. When she heard that I was an Indian research scholar and I lived in the USA and France, she suggested that it would be inspiring for the students if I shared some of my life experiences with them. She asked me if I could give a talk to the students on Monday.

I took a moment to reflect on what she was asking me for.

I felt very flattered and excited but also humbled and nervous all at the same time. I never gave a talk based on my life; neither did I give a motivational talk to high school students before.

I thought it would be an interesting experience for me and perhaps helpful for the students as well. So I said yes.

At the end of the day, I was surrounded by a bunch of students. They were curious about me. They never saw an Indian before.

They wanted to talk to me but they could not speak in English. On the other hand I could not speak Portuguese. So we ended up using some words in English, some in Spanish and some in Portuguese to try to communicate.

There was a brave and self confident boy among them. He proudly pointed to the girl standing beside him and told me:

"My girlfriend."

I could tell that he was a very talkative boy but he could not speak in English. He wrote something in his phone, used the internet to translate it in English and showed me:

"My English is shit."

This idea was taken up by a few others to help them convey what they wanted to tell me. Being the center of attraction made me feel very special. But there was a lot more of that to come.

The photo session
They never saw an Indian before!

On Sunday evening, Hérica brought her laptop. I spent a couple of hours putting together a power point presentation. I put on some pictures representing Indian culture. Then I added something about my childhood, college life in Bombay, graduate student life in the USA, my research interests, contributions to science, post doctorate work and cultural experiences in Paris. Then I included something about my journey through South America and finally, as requested by Hérica, some inspirational messages for the students.

I used the internet to translate the texts from English to Portuguese and Hérica edited them.

On Monday morning I was welcomed in Fundação Bradesco. I was invited to eat breakfast with the teachers. Most of them were young ladies. I managed to have small talks with some of them.

Afterward, I followed Hérica to a small classroom packed with more than sixty students (for the talk, two classes joined into one). As I entered the classroom I waved my arms to them and they responded with a loud concerted cheer. How thrilling! They already knew me and obviously liked me.

I asked the students if they preferred the talk to be delivered in English or Spanish, really hoping that they would choose English. But their choice was unequivocally Spanish.

I felt transfixed for a moment.

I never took a class or any formal lesson in Spanish. Before starting my journey I learned a little bit using the internet. Then in Peru I learned some Spanish words and expressions because I had to speak with people for basic necessities. But my Spanish was nowhere close to the level necessary to give a lecture in front of a class. In any case, I did not have the time to think. I pulled myself together as I had no other choice. I thought it would be like another adventure. I was getting used to encountering strange and difficult situations as they kept appearing since the beginning of my trip.

I took a deep breath and introduced myself using a few sentences in Spanish and the first slide of my presentation. I was not sure if the students understood anything. Nothing could be read from their faces.

But Hérica understood me. She followed my short speech with a detailed explanation in Portuguese. What a relief! We went on like that for all the slides. It was a talk about myself and I spoke rather in a modest way. But Hérica added her own comments and elaborations with an aim to impress and inspire the students about my qualifications and achievements. She stressed the importance of taking one's own decisions and putting *learning* over *money* and *fame* as the highest priority in life.

Team work

Hérica not only translated my speech but also made the best out of it.

When I showed them some pictures of my travel and told them that I was planning to write a book about it, they told me that they would buy my book when it comes out.

On the last slide I had some personal advise for the students:

1. Be brave to pursue your own interests and dreams, don't live a life as expected by others.
2. Don't blindly follow what is considered to be *cool* by the people around you.
3. Personally verify the truth about what you are told.
4. Explore! We live in a world with boundless knowledge, beauty and possibilities; one must explore to live a fulfilling life.

5. Have faith in yourself, at least try before you fail. You can do much more than you think you can.

6. Never give up, keep going!

Hérica conveyed the messages with her remarkable pedagogical skills. She made the best out of the presentation and made me feel proud of myself.

what is the joke about?

I did not always understand what the jokes were all about. Nevertheless I had fun.

The effect of the presentation on the students was evident and very flattering for me. At the end of the talk they cheered, thanked and congratulated me. Everybody wanted to take pictures with me. They joined me individually or in small groups to pose in front of multiple cameras. This went on for a while. They made me feel like a star.

It even went a bit too far. A boy requested an autograph from me. Some girls asked if I was already married. A girl quickly stole a touch from me to check if I was real and for good luck.

I and Hérica had to repeat the presentation in three more classes. The responses from the students were similarly overwhelming and flattering. At the end of the day, the director Marta congratulated us for doing a great job and expressed her gratitude.

That was such an unexpected and unforgettable

experience. Hérica Michelly made me a celebrity, for a day!

Surrounded
A memorable day in my life

FINALLY IN BOLIVIA

I spent five days in Rio Branco before heading back to Brasiléia. After collecting the police verification certificate, I applied for the visa for Bolivia and got it in two days.

I crossed that little bridge at the border again, showed my visa and finally got into Bolivia.

After spending a night in Cobija, a town at the border, I took a bus for a long and strenuous journey to Riberalta, a town at the crossroads in the Amazon. It was the same Amazon basin but the Bolivian part was underdeveloped compared to the Brazilian part. The road was unpaved for the most part and any vehicle moving on it created a dense trail of dust. Everything and everyone in the bus got covered in dust soon. There was no air conditioner in the bus and it was hot, I mean really hot.

On our way, we crossed Rio Madre de Dios, the same river that I met in Peru before. This river eventually meets the Amazon river and goes a long way to the Atlantic ocean. The bus was transported on a big flat boat across the river while we enjoyed the scenery outside.

I stayed one night in Riberalta. Although situated by the side of a river, the town had scarcity of running water. On the other hand it had a big beautiful plaza flooded with powerful lights in the night.

I noticed that the Bolivians thought of me as another Bolivian with more certainty than the Peruvians thought that I was another Peruvian. On a typical day in Bolivia, somebody would approach me and casually start talking to me about something without noticing that I did not understand a thing about what he or she said or joked about. My typical reaction with a smiling face was probably misleading, specially for the latter case. It encouraged them to talk even more. When I would finally be compelled to say something in broken Spanish in order to avoid being perceived as rude, he or she would give me a strange look, as if thinking "I wonder which part of Bolivia this strange guy comes from that he cannot even speak normal Spanish."

From Riberalta, I took an overnight bus to Rurrenabaque, a picturesque little riverside village in the Amazon. There I could see the tourists again, after a long time since I left Puerto Maldonado in Peru.

I stayed in Hostal Touristica Santa Ana which was simple and affordable. The hostel rather looked like a mini botanical garden with beautiful local plants. The garden was crisscrossed by footpaths made of a mosaic of colorful stones. There were plenty of hammocks and reclining chairs around. The room was small but clean and carefully designed for access to natural light and air. Through the window of my room, I could see many birds playing in the branches of the trees outside. There was a great variety of birds in that area.

When I arrived in Rurrenabaque I knew that I was going to stay there for a while. I was exhausted from the hectic journey and my arm got injured while trying to put on my backpack. On top of that I got food poisoning.

So I stayed there in Rurrenabaque, resting, healing and recharging my spirit. Ten peaceful days passed by.

The river village
A view of Rurrenabaque from the hilltop.

From Rurrenabaque, I started an eighteen hour long bus journey to reach La Paz, a big city in the Andes. It was time to say goodbye to the Amazon and get up in the high hills again.

The bus journey was like a ride in the elevator for a fast gain of height. It was a strenuous journey and I did not get much sleep in the night. However, in the morning I was rewarded with the panoramic views of the *Andes* as the bus made its way up to the Altiplano (highland).

We arrived in La Paz around six in the morning when the city was sleeping. La Paz looked like a modern city with skyscrapers and hills. The hills were covered with dense settlements all the way up to the tips. Except the Manhattan-like central part, the rest of the city looked like a big slum.

I checked into a hostel and tried to get some sleep.

Climbing from the low Amazon basin up to a height of 3650 meters gave me a *soroche* (altitude sickness). I could finally sleep a little bit but felt a headache when I got up.

I got out for lunch and walked up the main street. In sharp contrast with the sleepy atmosphere early in the morning, the city was bustling with people. The school kids, college students, office goers and many other busy-looking people hurriedly walked on the overcrowded sidewalks. I was overwhelmed by the brisk urban atmosphere, a sudden change from the slow and serene life in the Amazon.

After a few minutes of awkwardness, my city instinct kicked in. I waded through the crowd with fierce efficiency, just like a typical day on a busy street in Kolkata.

Bolivia still retains most of its indigenous people. I gaped at the typical round-shaped faces of hundreds of Bolivians as they passed by me. They were dressed in western style except a few women wearing their traditional bowler hats, plaited hairs and colorful *mantas* (shawl) and *polleras* (pleated-skirts).

The next day, I went on a day trip organized by the hostel to see the Tiahuanaco or Tiwanaku ruins near the southern shore of Lake Titicaca.

Tiwanaku is one of the most important pre-Columbian sites in Bolivia. Thousands of years before the birth of Christ, some tribes of native Americans abandoned their traditional hunter-gatherer lifestyle, adopted agriculture and settled near lake Titicaca. These initial settlements gradually expanded with time and became the birthplace of the Tiwanaku Civilization. The Tiwanakus built up an empire covering some parts of present day Bolivia, Peru and Chile.

The high period of the civilization was approximately between 500 AD and 900 AD. After that it collapsed probably due to drastic climate change. A few centuries after that the Inca civilization was born.

A monolithic structure made by the Tiwanaku people
This one looks similar to the Bennet monolith.

In the Lithic Museum, we saw a colossal monolithic statue. It is called Bennet monolith, named after its discoverer. It is more than 7 meters high and weighs about 20 tons, the largest Andean statue discovered so far. The monolith shows a man wearing a mask, belt and a skirt, holding a cup on his one hand and a tablet on the other, as if ready for an offering to the divine. The body is covered with mysterious symbols and figures related to Tiwanaku mythology and astronomy.

After the museum, we visited Akapana, a cross shaped pyramidal structure. The major part of the pyramid is still buried under the ground. Excavating and reconstructing a large archeological ruin like Akapana requires a lot of money and resources. The good news is that UNESCO declared Tiwanaku as a world heritage site. We can hope that more facts about the Tiwanaku civilization will be available to us in the future. I thought that it would be interesting to revisit the site in a few decades.

The gate of the sun
A monolithic structure.

Next we saw the Puerta del Sol (gate of the sun), another big monolithic structure. There was a face carved in the middle of the top part of the gate. The face was surrounded by some enigmatic figures. The interpretations of these figures and symbols are still under debate.

The monolithic structures on the site were carved out of single blocks of stones that were transported from stone quarries several kilometers away. It was an exceptional feat achieved by human muscle power since they did not have any large animals to haul those huge and heavy stones.

Alien invasion?
Temple with mysterious faces.

Next we saw a temple with many human faces carved on the walls. Each face captured a different gesture, emotion or mood. Many of the faces were grotesquely distorted. Our tour guide told us that some TV channel made a show claiming that some of those faces were of aliens.

Our last site was Pumapunku, a temple complex

mostly hidden under ground. The excavated objects included many stone blocks with different symbols carved in with remarkable precisions. The plane surfaces, the angles and the straight lines were so accurate that not even a razor blade could fit in the joints between the stones.

The stone blocks were held together by *I* shaped clamps made of bronze. The precision and knowledge of geometry behind these stonework are startling even to the modern world. Many speculations are offered to explain the techniques behind these outlandish pieces of work. In many ways the stonework of Tiwanaku people was superior to that of the Incas who were their descendants.

Precision perfect
Making such highly accurate stonework is very difficult even with modern technology.

I came back to La Paz with my mind lost in the thoughts of ancient Tiwanaku civilization. Many mysteries about this civilization are still buried under the ground, waiting for us to uncover some day.

I left La Paz for Oruro, a highland city famous for its colorful carnivals. It was not the season for carnivals but I decided to visit it anyway. It was a convenient stopover to go to Uyuni, my next destination.

I went to see the zoo of *Oruro* in a sunny but sleepy afternoon. I was one of the few visitors in the little zoo. When I was buying the ticket for the entrance, a Bolivian girl and a man who worked in the zoo got interested in me. As usual, they never met an Indian before.

They asked me many questions about India. They even called the manager of the zoo. He came over, introduced himself and treated me like a special guest. He told me a bit about the history of the zoo.

After the manager finished his welcome speech and went away I started exploring the zoo. For the first time in my life I saw the condors, one of the largest birds in the world. When the condors spread their wings, they looked so gigantic, so unreal, like some monstrous creature described in the book *Gulliver's Travel.* Although they were put in a huge cage, it seemed very small when they flew circling inside it. I was thrilled to see their majestic flights.

When I was a child, I was fascinated by reading an article about armadillos and seeing a picture of one of them. In the Oruro zoo, I saw them alive for the first time. Like rats, they busily crawled on the mud using their little paws.

Ricardo, the manager of the hotel was a very warm, caring and interesting man in his thirties. It was the off season in *Oruro* and I was the only guest in the hotel. Ricardo and his wife lived on the top floor of the building.

There was a dining area on the top floor where I had my breakfast every morning. Ricardo prepared my breakfast with a lot of care. I felt the comfort of home and had the most satisfying conversation with him that I could manage with my level of Spanish. With more practice, I was getting more confident with the language.

"Obaidur, how do you like Bolivia?" –asked Ricardo.

"I like it very much. I especially like that the Bolivians love their ancient cultures and are successful in keeping them alive. I noticed that some Bolivians still wear their traditional clothes. I saw this more often in Bolivia than in Peru and Brazil."

"I am glad to hear that you like Bolivia. Did you see any of the archeological sites in Bolivia yet?"

"Yes, I saw the Tiwanaku ruins near La Paz. I was really amazed by it. To tell you the truth, I found it no less interesting than Machu Picchu. It is a pity that the site is visited only by a handful of tourists while Machu Picchu is infested by them."

"It is a pity, indeed. You know, only a small fraction of that site is uncovered so far. The vast majority is still under the ground. But our government is callous about it and does not take the necessary steps to protect the site, reconstruct it and make it more attractive to the tourists."

"It would be great if they did. People would get to know more about Bolivia and its ancient culture. It can also significantly help the economy."

"Yes, of course! But I get amazed by what they are doing with it instead. Now that UNESCO declared it a world heritage site, there is some hope. But I am skeptic about how much work will be done in reality."

"You know I lived in France for a while and travelled in some other European countries. I was very impressed by the way they took care of their archaeological sites and got huge benefits out of them."

"So I heard. How did you like living in Europe?"

"I enjoyed living there very much. Travelling and exploring different cultures and histories made me feel very enriched. I would highly recommend you to visit Europe."

"I would love to, someday. So you want to live in Europe or you want to go back to India and settle there?"

"Well, I did not decide about that yet. It will depend on many things like where I get a job. How about you? Do you ever think about going to another country? Probably there is a better future for you in another South American country?"

"Yes, it could be. But you know Obaidur, I like it here. There might not be a lot of opportunities and development in Bolivia, but it has all that is very dear to me. It has its natural beauty, its culture, its people, its rich and ancient history. I like the simple way of living in Bolivia, living in close connection and harmony with nature, celebrating the culture that is our own, sharing our lives with our loved ones. I do not aspire for a career or earning a lot of money. Those other things are more valuable for me."

He was in love with the place where he grew up. He understood its true value.

I took a train from Oruro to reach Uyuni through the highlands. It was one of the luxurious train journeys in Bolivia. The train went through a surreal, desert-like landscape. There were no plants to see except some shrubs and grasses.

I saw small groups of simple huts scattered in the ghostly deserted land. I tried to imagine the daily lives of the inhabitants of those huts. They probably walked several miles to fetch water, spent a lot of time out in the open talking to each other and watching the stars.

When the Incas and later the Spanish conquistadors invaded the land, the aboriginal people were forced to live in the remote and inhospitable areas in the Altiplano. Some of those inhabitants are still surviving in the remotest and harshest areas. They still speak their ancestral languages which are long forgotten in the rest of the land.

They are the living fossils of the pre-Inca civilization.

I pondered over the idea of getting off the train and living with those inhabitants for a few days and learn about their unique ways of life. But I did not have the courage to act on the idea.

PLANET OF SALT

Salares, the world's largest salt plane spread over thousands of square kilometers, is a major tourist attraction in Bolivia. It was formed by some prehistoric lakes that dried out and left a few meters thick salt deposit at the bottom.

At Uyuni, I booked a three day long tour to explore the Salares with five other tourists.

We all got in a jeep early in the morning. Our driver cum guide was Ilario, a young but experienced local man. He was chubby, jolly and sometimes a bit silly. He did not speak much English but that was not a big problem. Soon, we started calling him Hilario as he cracked a lot of jokes and tried to sing English songs with his funny Spanish accent.

There was an Indian guy named Nikhil among the fellow travelers. He was the first Indian I met during my travel in South America. Nikhil was not only an Indian but also a Bengali like me.

It was a bit strange at first but very enjoyable to talk in Bengali so far away from home. Soon we started using a lot of slangs while talking. After a long and difficult period of communicating in Spanish, regaining the ability to speak fast and being perfectly understood was very gratifying.

Nikhil lived in Netherlands for more than ten years and had a Dutch citizenship. During his travel in South America it saved him from all the visa related problems that I had to face. Most of the times, he could just arrive at the border of a country and get a visa stamp on his passport and enter without any hassle.

Need some salt?
The Salar in Bolivia.

There was a young couple in the group, a boy from Scotland and a girl from Ireland. They had been backpacking around the world for fourteen months when I met them. During my trip, I met many people who were on long journeys, but nobody was travelling for such a long time. They seem to be still very energetic and enjoying the trip. A girl from New Zealand and another girl from Germany completed the group.

Within a few hours, we reached the Salar. The road that we were following literally disappeared. The jeep ran on the hard ground of salt, passing through a featureless, out of the world, blindingly white landscape. We were warned to protect our eyes with sun glasses.

Whichever direction I looked at, I only saw a flat land covered with salt. There was almost no variation of colors. There were no grasses, no trees, no animals, no houses, nothing except salt and the hills scattered faraway and the grey sky above. It was a desert land.

We conquered the Salar
Well, not quite! Apparently there was another Indian who got there before me and put the Indian flag.

Since we got in the jeep, my fellow passengers excitedly talked about taking pictures in the Salar using optical illusions. On the walls of the tourist office and the hostel, I saw many pictures of people on the salt plane in strange and creative poses. Since there are no trees or any other objects on the Salar to form a background, a person who is standing faraway can appear to be smaller in size but at the same distance as a person standing close to the camera. So if the person at the front holds her palm in a horizontal position, the person faraway can appear to be standing on it, as if shrunken by some black magic. To take countless fun pictures by exploiting this optical illusion is one of the main tourist activities in the Salar.

No need for Photoshop
Creating an illusion in the Salar.

We were no exception to the norm. We stopped on our way to take some pictures. Using the illusion, we stood on a bottle of wine, carried somebody on a finger and threw somebody by blowing air from the mouth. Our minds raced on to think of many such ideas.

Who is taller?
Or shall I rather ask how many times taller?

Next, we stopped to see the Isla del Pescado (island of the fish). It was an island covered by corals when the lake was filled with water. These days it appears like a small hill rising from the endless plane of salt. I took a close look at the rocks of the island and noticed that the original rocks were wrapped with layers of rocks formed by the corals. The two types of rocks had different colors and textures making it easy to distinguish.

The height of the island made me realize that we had been driving on the bottom of a lake that once contained an enormous volume of water. I could visualize, the dark bottom as seen from the surface of the water, colorful fish playing and feeding near the corals, many other strange creatures swimming in the water.

The hill was covered by colossal cacti, many times taller than my own height. We climbed up the hill to enjoy the breathtaking view of the dreamlike white land and faraway hills. Occasional winds blew snow-white salt over the ground.

As the day grew older, a strong and bitingly cold wind started to blow. To spend the night, we were taken to a hut on the foot of a hill. After getting out of the jeep, we quickly pulled down our luggage and ran inside the hut to save ourselves from being frozen or blown away by the erratic wind. It took just a few minutes but it was enough to give me the chills in my bones. The hut looked very primitive but it protected us from the winds. We felt a great relief hiding in the tiny hut in the middle of the inhospitable and bleak salt-land all around us. We were like a group of human explorers on the planet of salt.

The walls of the hut were made of blocks of salt-stone dug out of the ground. We huddled around a table made of salt and sat on blocks of salt instead of chairs. We were given hot tea to keep us warm while we waited for the dinner to be cooked and served.

The Irish girl pulled out a stack of playing cards. We

played card games and shared stories of our journeys. Soon, everybody was in a joyous mood.

I was sitting with my face toward the windows. From time to time I was catching some glimpses from outside. All of a sudden, I saw something shining on the horizon. Initially I thought it was a light from another hut. But with time it started to get bigger and stronger.

I got curious and drew everyone's attention to it. Soon we realized that it was the moon rising on the horizon. It grew bigger and bigger gradually washing away the mystical darkness around it. Finally it became a big round moon. The soft moonlight washed the white salt-land with a milky glow. That was one of the most outlandish phenomena I had ever experienced.

We all went outside ignoring the wind. Everybody got their cameras out to capture the moments. I rather absorbed everything with my eyes. I did not believe in the possibility of capturing such a wonder of nature with a camera.

We got up early in the morning and saw the sunrise. But it was not as exciting as the moonrise in the previous night.

After a quick breakfast we started our journey. Hilario continuously chewed coca leaves while driving. The white landscape of the Salar was soon replaced by hills and highlands. Each turn around a hill revealed a new type of geography and beauty. The road was unpaved, wavy and full of round pebbles. But we had a powerful jeep and Hilario drove it fast. Usually, we passed by a hill within a few minutes of its appearance on the horizon.

On our way, we saw some large rocks oddly scattered on a sandy desert-like landscape. The black rocks appeared to be misplaced as they were in sharp contrast with the color and texture of the background. Hilario told us that the bizarre landscape was named after Salvador Dali, the Spanish painter renowned for his surrealist paintings.

A bit farther, we saw wild vicuñas grazing on the highland. Vicuñas are closely related to llamas and alpacas. We stopped the jeep to see them from close and take some pictures but they did not like to be near people. I tried to sneak up on them but they did not give me a chance. I had to be satisfied zooming with my camera.

As we climbed four thousand meters above the sea level, it started to get bitterly cold and windy.

Next we stopped to see a dormant volcano. It was standing proudly in front of us like a giant cone with its peak high up in the air. Hilario told us that climbing the hill to the top was one of the common tourist activities. Since our package did not include that activity, we moved on.

Farther on, we stopped at several lakes with intense colors and unearthly beauty. I wanted to just stand there and gaze at those tranquil lakes forever. But the fiercely cold wind forced me to get back to the jeep.

Unreal!
The landscapes looked like desktop backgrounds

At noon, we stopped for lunch at lake Laguna Colorada (red lagoon). Due to sedimentation and some algae, the lake had patches of red among other colorations in its water. Hundreds of pink flamencos were feeding in the shallow but enormous lake. I saw clusters of pink dots scattered over a vast region on the colorful waters of the lake with a panoramic background of electric blue sky and snow-top hills. The air was fresh. The day was bright. That was a precious moment of coming face to face with the pristine and rare beauty of nature.

The pink dots
Hundreds of Flamencos that looked like pink dots from far.

After finishing our lunch, we entered the Eduardo Avaroa National Park. We got a shelter in one of the park's residences. It was time to unpack, freshen up and take rest.

The night was freezing. There was no hot water in the facility. After having some pasta for dinner, we and all other tourists huddled around a fire while some played the guitar.

On the last day of our trip, we got up at four thirty in the morning, ate some pancakes and hopped in the jeep. A long day was ahead of us.

Hilario drove the jeep to an ever increasing height. We reached over five thousand meters above sea level, my personal best.

After a few hours of driving, we stopped to see a geyser, basically a hole in the ground that continuously blew hot steam. Several active volcanoes used to be there in the past but one can only see some geysers and hot springs now.

Next we stopped at a hot spring. A small bathtub was filled with the warm water coming from the spring. But it was on the open ground unprotected from the cold wind that was blowing over it. Initially we were reluctant to take off our warm clothes and change into swimming clothes. But one by one we got enough courage to do that in lightening speed and jump in the hot tub. Once we were in the warm water, nobody wanted to get out.

Around noon four members of the group were dropped off at the border so that they could continue their journey into Chile. Even though we spent only three days together, I felt like I was saying goodbye to some old friends.

It took another five hours to drive back to Uyuni. Hilario constantly chewed coca leaves while driving. Chewing coca leaves helps to stay alert and it numbs the feeling of hunger and cold. I felt very grateful to him because he drove us through the rough highlands of Bolivia for three days in a row. His work was physically very strenuous.

Although, I just sat in the jeep for the whole time, I realized how exhausted I was when I got back to Uyuni. I gave Hilario a good tip, shook his big hand and slowly started walking toward my hostel.

As I tried to look back, the whole experience seemed like a dream.

BIZARRE LANDSCAPES AND LAKE TITICACA

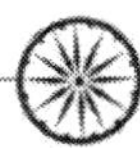

I left Uyuni, a ghostly windy town for a warm and beautiful little city called Tupiza in the south of Bolivia. I was supposed to reach Tupiza at 1 am or so I was told. But the bus dropped me there at 4 am instead, something not so uncommon in Bolivia.

The bus stand was gloomy and almost empty. As I walked toward the street, I felt that I was being watched by a man sitting on the bench. Very suspicious. Thieves and robbers probably prowled that bus stop at such an ungodly hour. I was completely vulnerable to any attack.

Fortunately, I had an online reservation for a hostel close to the bus stop. I just needed to find it. But there was nobody on the street to ask for direction. I was afraid of talking to a stranger anyway.

So I took the main street and started walking on it. I had the address and I knew that the hostel was very close to the station. As I walked fast to get inside the hostel as soon as possible, somebody called me from behind.

I knew, I was in trouble. I pretended that I did not hear the call and kept walking. But the call was repeated. I instinctively raised the pace of my walk. A moment later, I heard somebody walking behind me. I was being pursued. I was horrified that somebody would jump on my back at any moment. Soon, a lanky man, closely resembling the Frankenstein's monster, caught up with me. He opened his mouth showing a set of large crooked teeth and asked me in Spanish:

"Do you have a reservation?"

"Yes" - I answered and continued walking without a delay. I wanted him to go away.

But that did not discourage him. He caught up with me again and showed me a small piece of paper. I could not believe my eyes when I saw my own name written on it. I wondered what kind of scam that could be.

I looked at him in bewilderment. I was not sure what to say. Then he broke it down to me. He told me that he was waiting at the bus stop to receive me on behalf of the hostel. I again checked the paper and saw that the name of the hostel was also written on it. The name did match with the one that I was looking for.

I thought about it for a moment and remembered that I mentioned the expected time of my arrival while booking the hostel. However, I did not expect anybody to meet me at the station.

He asked me to follow him to the hostel. Half minded, I started walking with him. I knew that the hostel was very close to the station. In case it took more than a couple of minutes, I was not going to continue to follow him.

It did not take long, at all. Just a few steps farther, he pointed his finger to a sign board hanging over the entrance of a building. I saw the name of the hostel written on it. He opened the gate and asked me to get in. I went through the gate slowly and hesitatingly, expecting an attack coming from any direction at anytime.

To my surprise, there was no attack. He showed me the room. It was a dorm room with four unoccupied single beds. It was clean, cozy and comfortable, something I badly needed after staying awake the whole night.

I went to bed still wondering about the unexpected late night reception.

~ • ~

In the morning, I went to the roof of the hostel to find myself in a small town closely surrounded by grey and red colored hills. The sky was bright and the air was warm, a great relief from the wind chill in Uyuni.

I went for a walk in the town. The narrow streets had many stores and restaurants on both sides. However, most of them had no customers.

On the street, I ran into an Uruguayan girl whom I met earlier in the hostel. We ended up having a chat in a café near the central plaza. I found out that she worked in the weather forecasting department in Uruguay. She told me about her six months long visit in Antarctica where she was the only girl in the camp. She also showed me some stunning pictures of Antarctica.

On the following day, I was ready for a hike.

I ate breakfast, packed lunch, took some water and started walking. For direction, I had a basic map provided by the hostel. After walking about two kilometers, I took a right turn at Palmira and entered a dry valley surrounded by hills with red rocks.

I heard that the valley was a popular place for horse riding. I also saw footprints and horse manure on the trail. So I expected to see many tourists mounted on horse backs. But after walking on a trail for a while I saw nobody, neither on a horse nor on foot.

The trail started to split and crisscross with other trails. There were no signs to mark the trails. So I followed the broadest trail and it took me a long way.

The complete silence and mars-like landscape of the valley had a strange effect on me. As I walked alone for a while, an eerie feeling possessed me. My awareness was dragged outside my body. I became aware of me as a separate being. I felt that the silent hills watched me as I passed by.

I snapped out of the dreamlike state when I saw a pile of trash randomly dumped on the ground. I saw more such piles by looking around. Piles of broken glasses, plastic bottles and other trash. Plastic bags flew around desecrating the beauty of the entire valley. Sad and disturbed, I kept walking.

The trail took me in a circuitous way. By that time I realized that I was lost. Finally, I ended up on a hillside overlooking a beautiful town.

I was thinking of going to the town and taking a break at a cafeteria when I saw two people walking on the trail, coming toward me. I felt joy in my heart to finally see some living creature in that lifeless desert-land.

I started a conversation with them. They were a French couple. It turned out that they were on a walk to see the same tourist attractions that I intended to see myself. However, they came from the town ahead of me. But I was very surprised when they told me that they also came from Tupiza and pointed in the direction of the town ahead. I had a hard time believing what I heard.

We were standing on the side of a small hill with a panoramic view of the town. When I saw the town carefully, I realized that the town was indeed Tupiza, seen at a different angle than the one from the roof of my hostel. The trail that I followed took me in a circle back to Tupiza.

In any case, we started walking together to look for the right destinations. After a little bit of wandering we found them.

The land was a laboratory of nature, full of curious geographical formations. The Puerta del Diablo (gate of the devil) was a gap between two huge flat rocks standing up vertically, just like walls. Numerous obelisk-shaped rocks rose to the sky at Valle de los Machos (valley of the machos). As we kept walking, the valley became narrower, ending in a canyon called Cañon del Inca (Canyon of the Incas). We ate our lunch there before heading back.

The gate of the devil
A strange rock formation

After enjoying a few warm days in Tupiza, I took an overnight bus to reach La Paz. Although I had visited La Paz already, I decided to take another break there because it was conveniently located on my way to Copacabana, my next destination.

I checked in the same hostel as the last time and went to see Valle de la Luna (Valley of the moon).

That was one of the strangest landscape I had ever seen. Among the hills, there was a large grey area that looked like the back of a porcupine, full of large needle-shaped rocks standing straight up. A walking trail was built over this natural amusement park. I walked for an hour in that wonderland.

The valley of the machos
Rocks with character

Copacabana was my next and last stop in Bolivia before I returned to Peru. It is a small town near lake Titicaca, the highest navigable lake in the world.

Valley of the moon
Not the best spot for landing a helicopter

A part of the journey from La Paz to Copacabana was through the hills dotted on the side of the lake Titicaca. As the bus took turns and moved from one hill to the other, I could appreciate the beauty of the lake from different standpoints. The misty mountains on the horizon, the white clouds, the blue sky and their reflections on the still water of the lake painted a spectacular landscape on the canvas of my bus window.

I did not want the journey to end.

But I realized that it was coming to an end when I saw the town approaching from far, Copacabana, stretched over the valley between two hills, on the bank of lake Titicaca.

I found a hotel called Residencial Paris. The name

immediately attracted me, as if the hotel was built for me, a former Parisian.

I got a room on the top floor. It was a tall building and there was no elevator. Climbing up the stairs to my room was like climbing up the Eiffel Tower. But it was rewarding. I could see the hills and a big part of the lake while sitting on my bed.

Deadly tired from the bus journey, I fell asleep in the afternoon and got up around midnight. When I stepped out of my room, it seemed very quiet and dark outside. I felt very hungry. So I got down the stairs to go out and find some food. I tried to open the main door of the hotel and found out that it was locked from inside. The noise woke up the caretaker. A moment later he appeared in front of me.

"Hello! Do you need to go out?", he asked me in Spanish.

"Hello!", I replied. "Yes, I need to buy some food."

"All the restaurants and stores in Copacabana are normally closed at this hour."

"Oh, really?", frustration was apparent in my voice.

"If you like, you can go out and check if something is still open".

When I got out, the main street looked nothing like what I saw during the day. The shutters of all the stores were closed, no cars or pedestrians were in sight, not even the dogs that were playing on the street before.

Hopeless, I got back into the hotel. I was about to climb the stairs to my room when the caretaker called me back. He told me:

"Copacabana is a small town. It is not full of tourists like in La Paz where the restaurants are open until late in the night."

"I see."

"I have some bread. Take them so that you will have something to eat."

He gave me some small breads. I expressed my thankfulness to him and gladly took the breads. This way he saved me from starving that night.

I was very touched by his hospitality. In fact, this was not a rare incidence. I was treated by many such acts of kindness during my stay in Bolivia. They always treated me like a fellow human being and not as a source of money. They freely expressed their emotions and feelings to me as if I was a close relative to them.

Picturesque
A view of Copacabana from hilltop

Most people in Bolivia lived their entire lives in hardship. But that did not harden their hearts. They were very human, thoughtful and down to earth. Their daily struggles enabled them to feel the suffering of a fellow human being. For them, life was not about accumulating and consuming a lot of materials. It was about being together, caring for each other and cherishing the simplest things.

I spent a whole day walking along the shore of the lake and hiking in the hills that surrounded Copacabana. Tiny settlements were scattered on the valleys between the hills. Even though I lived in big cities most of my life, I always felt a strong connection with the rural existence. The wide open sky, the trees trembling by the wind, the small huts, the llamas grazing on the ground, the peasants working on the fields, all that made me feel very secure, free and happy.

Isla del Sol (Island of the sun) is a small island in lake Titicaca, very close to Copacabana. According to Inca mythology, the first Inca Manco Capac and his sister-wife Mama Cello were created in that island. It was Manco Capac who later founded Cuzco and built the powerful Inca empire. This island is also the birthplace of the Sun god.

I arrived at the island from Copacabana by an hour long boat ride. From far, the island looked like a couple of rugged rocks sharply rising from the water.

I got off the boat and started climbing a dizzyingly steep stairway made by blocks of stones. The stairway later turned into a trail, still going up the hill. It took me through a little village called Yumani.

It was a village frozen in time.

It appeared to me that the villagers lived in a way similar to the Incas hundreds of years ago. They wore very simple traditional clothes. The houses were made of large blocks of stones. They grew vegetables on the flat terraces cut on the steep hills. Herds of llamas, sheep and donkeys were kept in the fenced front and back yards of the houses.

Never in my life did I think that I would stay in such a village.

It took me about forty five minutes to climb up to the top of the hill. As soon as I got there, I was approached by a five or six years old boy. He took me to a small hotel nearby. The hotel consisted of a few simple rooms, owned and managed by a family that lived in a hut on the backside. The hotel seemed to be recently constructed and the rent was very little.

I checked in the hotel and went out for lunch. On a trail along the edge of the hill, I found a restaurant with hilltop lake view. I ate some fish for lunch while savoring the gorgeous view of the lake from the window.

But the view from my hotel room was even better. The hotel was perfectly located at the tip of the hill. It had two windows on the opposite walls through which I could see two sides of the lake while sitting on my bed. On one side, the snow peaks of the mountain Cordillera Real were visible between the blue lake below and blue sky above. They were outlandishly glowing in the evening light. White clouds covered the base of the mountain. The juxtaposition of them all created a visual aberration. The mountain appeared to be floating in the sky on top of the clouds. From the other window, I saw the sun setting on the lake. The water and the sky were colored with various shades of pink. I silently sat on my bed, watching.

The hotel owners also owned a few donkeys. Throughout the day and even in the night I heard shrill donkey calls, as if they were kept for announcing the hours. Although the village looked extraordinarily primitive at the first sight, it had all the facilities for the tourists: electricity, running water, small shops, hotels and restaurants. I thought it was some kind of a prank when I saw a signboard with *Internet* written on it.

~ • ~

The next day I started early to see the archeological sites of the island. The only way to explore the island was by walking on the trails made by the Incas. Perhaps that was a bit inconvenient for a lot of people but walking was my favorite mean of transportation. Specially getting a chance to walk on the Inca trail was titillating.

I hiked through the valleys, the beaches, the hills and some small settlements. The views were magnificent and the atmosphere was serene in the complete absence of any motor vehicles, industries or large populations.

Alike
A timeless moment in Isla del Sol

It took me about three hours to reach the northern part of the island. There was a very small archeological museum in the village Challa Pampa. It displayed the artifacts discovered by underwater excavations near a small island at the northern part of Isla del Sol. Many of those objects belonged to the Incas. Some of them were dated to an even earlier period of the Tiwanaku civilization. They suggest the influence of the Tiwanaku civilization over the lake Titicaca region before the rule of the Incas.

Other archeological discoveries suggested human existence in that region a few thousand years before the birth of Christ. Perhaps, many other mysteries are hiding at the bottom of the lake to be discovered some day.

A labyrinth like structure called Chinkana is one of

the few Inca ruins in the island. The significances and functions of these ruins are not well understood until today.

Ancient conference room?
Ceremonial table, the functions of these structures are still debated

I had a long walk on the Inca trail back to the south part of the Island. The trail went along the tops of the hills with breathtaking views of the lake on all sides. As the sun went down slowly, I kept pondering about the Incas who walked on the same trail hundreds of years ago.

I felt sad to leave the beautiful, foggy and mysterious island, Isla del Sol.

Chinkana
An Inca temple

Walk to the sky
A walk on the Inca trail has a soothing effect on the soul

FROM THE DESERT TO THE COAST

I took a bus from Copacabana and crossed the border to Puno, Peru. Another bus took me from Puno to Arequipa, the second largest city in Peru. Again it felt a bit strange to walk on the crowded streets of Arequipa after such a peaceful time in Copacabana and Isla del Sol.

However, the broad streets and specially the central plaza created a cool and welcoming atmosphere. The big and beautiful cathedral on the side of the plaza covered a big part of the sky. The volcanoes Chachani and El misty could be seen behind it. I spent one day exploring the city.

Some of the deepest canyons in the world can be found near Arequipa. I went on a package tour with a few other travelers to see one of the canyons. A van picked us from the city and took us on a long ride to the canyon. Then we took a trail to get all the way down to the bottom of the canyon. We spent two nights in two different huts along the river.

The canyon was inhabited by human settlers thousands of years ago. The remnants of their experiments with agriculture are still visible in that region.

On the last day, we started early in the morning for a steep climb of more than one thousand meters. In a few hours we were all up. On our way back to Arequipa, we stopped for lunch and a bath in a hot spring.

A ten hour long bus trip took me from Arequipa to Nazca through the desert along the coast. The ghostly sand dunes and the misty water of the pacific ocean were all that I could see on the way.

Nazca is known for its geoglyphs, one of the archeological mysteries in the world. These geoglyphs consist of some enigmatic lines, geometrical shapes and figures of some animals drawn on the desert, spanning over several hundred kilometers. They can be best seen from the sky. There is a lot of speculations about the meaning and significance of these drawings which were created by the people of Nazca, a pre-Inca civilization.

Immediately after checking in the hostel, I went to attend a talk about the Nazca lines in the planetarium inside hotel Nazca Lines. The presenter was an old man, very knowledgeable and passionate about the history of the archaeological site.

I learned many interesting things about Nazca lines from him.

Maria Reiche, a German mathematician, archeologist and a pioneer in the research on Nazca lines lived in the hotel and surveyed the area. She was amazed by the high mathematical precisions of the geometrical figures and noticed their curious astronomical significances.

Starting from 1940, Maria Reiche spent many decades in Nazca deciphering the mysteries of the lines. She had to work alone in the desert for many hours observing the lines with her bare eyes. She published her work in a book titled *The Mystery on the Desert* that generated international attention to Nazca lines. Throughout the rest of her life she passionately fought for the preservation of the site and generating public awareness. In her later ages she suffered from skin disease, lost her eye sight and died of cancer at the age of 95. She was buried near Nazca with honor and respect.

The Nazca lines had some unique features. Many of the geoglyphs depicting animals were constructed by a single line without intersecting with itself. On the other hand, some geometrical figures had many lines intersecting at a single point. In order to construct the lines, the dark colored rocks from the desert surface were removed to expose the light colored rocks underground. The widths of the lines were between a few centimeters to a few feet and the depths were about a few centimeters.

The Nazca lines were constructed by several generations of people over many centuries. Their motivations for drawing them could have been different. Rainfall in Nazca is extremely rare. Thus, water had been a very important factor for the survival of the ancient people living there. Many of the lines in the desert lead up to sources of water coming down the hills. Some experts speculated that religious believes related to the availability of water had been a major motivation for the construction of the lines.

There are several other speculations about the meaning and significance of the lines. However, the scarcity of archaeological evidence makes it difficult to establish a concrete theory. Many groups are actively pursuing research in Nazca and new structures continue to be discovered.

After the talk I returned to the hostel, booked a plane ride to see the Nazca lines and went to bed, tired but excited.

•

Next day morning, a taxi took me to a small airport specifically built for exploring Nazca lines from the air.

When I got inside the small aircraft, I met three other passengers, a pilot and a co-pilot all crammed in there. Pretty soon we were in the air.

I looked down at the beautiful green landscape which transformed into a featureless desert. In a few minutes, mysterious lines crisscrossing the land started to appear.

Among the lines was the pan-American highway, oddly cutting through the land. Sadly, it was built before the significance of the lines was discovered and publicized.

Each passenger was given a map showing the track of the plane through the selected geoglyphs to observe. Whenever a geoglyph appeared, the pilot tilted the plane over one side and circled over it so that the passengers sitting on that side could get a good view of the structure. Then he tilted it over the other side for the benefit of the passengers on that side.

During the 30 minutes ride we saw the drawings of a whale, an astronaut, a monkey, a dog, a hummingbird, a spider, a condor, a heron bird, a tree and finally a pair of giant hands with a total of nine fingers on them. It was thrilling to imagine that those lines were made by people who lived more than a thousand years in the past.

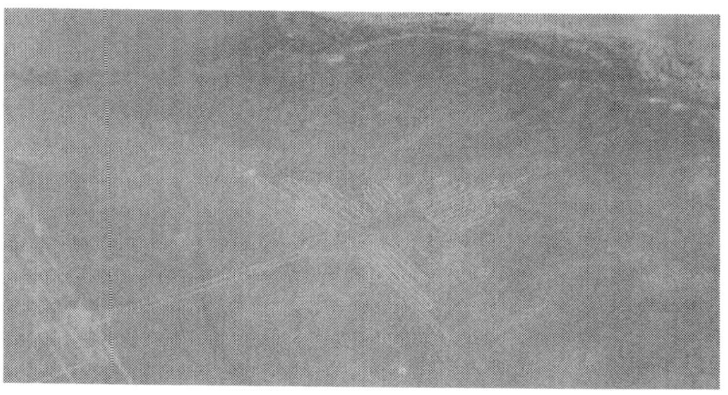

The hummingbird
A geoglyph in Nazca

The tree and the hands
The pan-American highway went through the area

There are theories that suggest connections between some of the structures and star constellations. For instance, the spider is associated with the Orion and the monkey with the big dipper.

Although I was fascinated by seeing the geoglyphs, I could not enjoy the plane ride very much. It was a bumpy ride and perhaps because of all the tilting and circling, I felt nauseated. I felt quite sick near the end of the ride and was relieved to be back and standing on the solid ground.

In the afternoon I went to another trip to see a necropolis (cemetery) of the Nazca people.

The necropolis displayed the interiors of a few graves. Mummified human bodies were kept in the fetal position as was the practice of the Nazca people. They were kept out in the open air without the confines of walls. Nazca is one of the driest places in the world. The bodies do not degrade in such dry climate.

Many broken pieces of bones were lying all over the

necropolis. It seemed that the ground went through some kind of upheaval in the past. I got to know that robbers and local people repeatedly excavated the necropolis in search of valuables.

The ancestors
Necropolis in Nazca

The Nazca people also built multi-level graves to bury the whole family. The levels were filled according to family status. The head of the family occupying the lowest level.

The archeologists excavating the graves found the mummy of a special man with very long hair and ceremonial clothing. It is speculated that the man was a shaman who conducted the rituals and worshiped the gods.

Before heading back to the hostel, I saw a beautiful sunset at the necropolis that is still preserving the memories of some people from a far forgotten past.

From Nazca, I took a bus to reach Ica, a city in the middle of the desert. I needed to take a taxi to go a short distance away from Ica to Huacachina. When I got off the bus, two taxi drivers approached me.

When I was getting inside one of the taxis, the other taxi driver asked me in Spanish, "Are you from India?"

I was pleasantly surprised at this. This was one of the rarest occasions in South America when somebody got this at the first guess.

I told him that I was indeed an Indian and I was very impressed by him.

Within a few minutes we got out of Ica and entered a world of sand. It felt like we were swimming in a sea with enormous waves of sand. But unlike the waves of water, the sand waves were stationary, or so I thought at that moment.

Within a few more minutes I was dropped at Huacachina, a charming oasis in the desert.

It was a tiny oasis with a little pond surrounded by a line of palm trees. Little birds were playing in the calm water of the pond. A warm breeze made tiny ripples on it and caressed the bare parts of my skin. The serenity of the place was contagious.

Hills of sand stood around the pond. The oasis looked strikingly out of place among the barren landscape of the desert. Before seeing it, I could not imagine such a beautiful oasis hidden behind the sand dunes.

Tourists visit Huacachina to enjoy the beauty of the oasis and savor the warm balmy weather, a great relief from the wet and cold climate of the coastal region.

The most popular tourist activities in Huacachina are sand boarding and buggy rides over the dunes. I had only one day to see Huacachina and I wanted to do something different. So, I decided to climb one of the dunes surrounding the pond.

As soon as I started climbing, I realized that it was going to be harder than what I thought it would be. My sandals turned out to be useless for climbing. I could not get any grip on the sand with them. So I took them off and started climbing barefoot.

Halcyon Huacachina
An oasis near Ica, Peru

It was not so bad at the beginning but soon the dune started to become steep. The fine sand felt very soft under my feet, rolling away as I put pressure on it. The climb became frustratingly slow. Every attempt of stepping up was followed by a down slide and digging of the foot into the sand, gaining about one third of the height aimed for.

I struggled on until the narrow tip of a dune, gasped for breathe, steadied myself on the ever sliding sand and looked around. As far as I could see, a bleak and barren sea of sand endlessly spread itself, unceremoniously meeting the grey sky on the horizon. A pale melancholic afternoon light gently slanted on the somber landscape.

Although the desert appeared to be static as

compared to the sea, I noticed that the wind was slowly blowing the sand over the surface. This process, given a long period of time, can move a mountain of sand. The desert looks static only to the eyes of impatient observers.

While I climbed through the side of the dune under its long shadow, the sand felt cool and soothing on my feet. But when I reached the sunlit top, the hot sand burned my feet. This was just the weak light of the late afternoon. How hot was the sand at noon?

Sliding sand dunes

Walking on desert sand is not as much fun as it looks like.

There was a larger dune that started from the top of the dune I was standing on. Soon I started climbing it through a narrow ridge that fell sharply on both sides. It was challenging to climb up the steep path by stepping on the ever sliding sand without falling down either side of the ridge.

Although I imagined that falling down the sand dune would not kill me, I was still afraid of the plunge. After a bit of struggle I gave up. That was enough for the day. I took a last look around and got down, down to the charming oasis.

I met a bunch of friendly travelers back in the hostel. In the evening I joined them for dinner in one of the few restaurants in the little oasis. Afterward, we went out for drinks.

Everybody was in a relaxed and joyous mood. We shared our stories and experiences. Among the people I met, Pablo interested me the most. He was in his forties with very short hair and an athletic body. Although he was the eldest person in the group he had an amazing ability to connect with the younger people without losing his mature behavior.

"So where are you from, Pablo?" - I wanted to know more about him.

"I was born and brought up in Nicaragua but I lived in Holland for the last fifteen years."

"How long have you been travelling?"

"About six months now, but I have a long way to go still. I am on a journey to see the whole world"

"Oh nice, which places did you visit so far?"

"Well, I started in Nicaragua, spent some time in Central America and then travelled in the north part of South America. Now I am in Peru and I will go south from here."

"Wow! You have spent *six months* seeing those parts? You must have really taken your time to explore everything. I am sure there are a lot of things to see in those regions."

"Yes, I am trying to cover as much as I can, taking time and experiencing different things on my way." - Pablo said with a smile.

"But this way, it might take many years for you to cover the whole world."

"I have time."

"You must have seen the Maya ruins in Central America. I am very eager to see them, but I am not sure if I will be able to make it this time." - I said excitedly.

"Yes, they are very interesting. You will surely like them."

"Ok, let me ask you a rather silly question. You must have had many wonderful experiences on your journey. So far, which one is the most memorable?"

"It is hard to pick one, of course. But I very much enjoyed the boat trip down the Amazon."

"Wow. I wanted to do that, but I did not have the time. How long was your trip?"

"A little more than two months."

"That is a long time. How was it? Didn't you get bored?

"No I did not. The journey was very relaxing. I loved watching the landscape pass by. The boat stopped regularly on its way to load and unload passengers and their children, luggage, cattle and various types of goods. In such a journey you really get to see the typical life of a local person."

"Sounds fascinating!"

"Yes, it is nice to have the time to do such things rather than visiting the touristy places only."

"I totally agree. So you do not have a job or a family back at home?"

"I am unmarried and I quit my job to be able to do what I am doing."

Pablo was the most committed traveler I met during my journey. He left behind what he had and set out to see the world. It must have taken many years to save enough money to support him during the journey. Some day when he will run out of money, he can go back and find another job.

•

The following day I checked out of the hostel and set off for Paracas, a touristy town at the coast of Pacific ocean. It was about an hour of bus journey from Huacachina. The climate of Paracas was very different from Huacachina. Bitingly cold and windy, it reminded me of Lima.

The hostel I checked in had a backyard right on the beach. It was inviting but at the same time disappointing since I could not imagine sitting there for ten minutes and not catching a cold.

Paracas is famous for its protected wildlife and national park. In the morning next day, I hopped on a motor boat packed with tourists clad in orange colored life jackets. In rocket speed, the boat headed toward an island named Ballestas.

Birds on the rocks
Due to the absence of land predators in these islands the birds can nest and breed peacefully in large numbers.

The island consisted of several small and big rocks steeply rising from the sea level. As we slowed down and approached the rocks, the ear splitting noise of the boat engine was replaced by a cacophony of thousands of sea birds of different species. Some were sitting on the rocks in large numbers, some were busily flying around and chasing each other and some were slowly gliding in the sky above.

Among many pelicans, cormorants and other species

of birds, our guide drew our attention to a small group of Humboldt penguins standing on the steep side of the rocks.

As the boat stealthily closed in, I looked up at those penguins with awe and disbelief. "Don't you have to go to Antarctica to see them?". Apparently not. They were right in front of my eyes, far away from Antarctica, flapping those exotic and unique wings.

We saw a few more groups of penguins as we started going around the island. "How could they climb such steep rocks?". I almost felt pity that they did not have the choice of flying like the other birds around them.

The guide told us that the penguins are very loyal birds, each penguin pairs up with a partner for life and lives alone when the partner dies.

A family of sea lions
Sea lions are related to seals. However, unlike seals, they can *walk* on land using their flippers.

I had hardly had the time to relax from the excitement of seeing penguins before I saw a bunch of sea lions basking on the rocks.

The blubbery bodies covered with brown colored fur, wobbled as they moved awkwardly on the rocks. They appeared like aliens. I would have been shocked to encounter them if I had not already seen them in pictures and documentaries.

On the other hand, the pair of large eyes and whiskers on the face made them look very familiar, just like pet dogs. Our small boat took us very close to them. Some of them looked at us. When I looked back at those big black eyes, I had a strange feeling inside me. I felt as if those innocent eyes were full of emotion, as if they could feel me, understand me. Even though their bodies looked unearthly but those looks were the looks of living creatures, of mammals, just like us.

The mating habit of sea lions is somewhat opposite of the mating habit of penguins. One male sea lion possesses and mates with eight to fifteen female sea lions. We could see many such groups lying on the rocks. In each group the large male could be easily distinguished from the much smaller females.

I wanted to see how they could climb up such steep rocks with their heavy and fluffy bodies. I could not catch one at the act of climbing but I saw some of them swimming in the semi-transparent, greenish, cold water. They swam skillfully, turning and twisting at an impressive speed. They were much more agile in water than on the rocks.

One male sea lion jumped in the water with a big splash right in front of our boat.

OVERCOMING THE SETBACKS

I arrived at Lima airport late in the afternoon. After checking in my bag I went through the security and reached the boarding area. While I was waiting there to get inside the plane, I heard an announcement:

"Obaidur Rahaman please contact the airport information desk."

"What now?". Sensing trouble, I went there. Two young Peruvian girls in their uniforms were standing behind the desk. We exchanged greetings.

"Can I see your passport please?" - asked one of the girls.

"Yes, sure." - I handed in my passport.

She flipped through the pages and asked:

"You are going to Mumbai, right?"

"Yes."

"And you are changing your flight at?"

"My first flight is until Madrid and then I will take a second flight to Mumbai." -I said calmly.

"Do you have a transit visa?"

"No. Do I need a transit visa? I have a waiting period of less than two hours."

"Yes, our record shows that you need a transit visa. It is required for an Indian passport holder."

"Really? I have less than two hours of waiting time and I am supposed to transfer in the same terminal. I don't need to go out of that area."

She kept searching my passport for the visa and when she could not find it she gave it to the tall girl standing beside her.

The tall girl also flipped through it as I stood there waiting. She told me:

"So you don't have any European visa?"

"No, I don't."

The two girls discussed about this among themselves for a bit and told me at the end:

"We will keep your passport to be checked by our staff. Please have a seat and do not leave this area. We will call you."

They showed me a bench within the restricted area. There was a middle aged man sitting on the bench already. He looked like an Indian.

"Are you an Indian?" -he asked me excitedly.

"Yes, and you are also an Indian?"

"Yes, haha...I saw you from far and I thought...ahhh, he looks like an Indian." - he said with a smile.

I smiled back. It felt good to meet an Indian. I said:

"I have been travelling in South America for four months and you are the only Indian I have met. I mean, I met a couple of other Indians but they have European citizenships."

"Yes, not many Indians come to South America."

"So you are here for travelling?"

"No, I came here for business. I come to Peru regularly for business."

"I see."

Soon I was called by an airport staff again. This time

it was a young man. He checked my passport one more time and told me:

"You do not have any European visa or USA visa in your passport?"

"No, I don't."

"Are you sure? Maybe it is in your old passport?"

"No. I had both European and USA visa before but they are not valid anymore. I did not know that I needed a transit visa."

"Well, we cannot let you board this plane. Please wait in that restricted zone. After the boarding, we will see what can be done."

So I sat there waiting while all the passengers including the Indian man went in the plane one by one. He wished me luck before he left. By that time it got dark outside.

When the last passenger was in and the gate was closed, I went back to the desk. The girls took my passport, made some phone calls and told me:

"We can send you to Mumbai through a different route, through South Africa."

"Okay, but did you check that I will not need a transit visa in South Africa?"

"Yes, we checked it. You will not need a visa there."

"Are you sure? Because I don't want to get stranded there in South Africa."

"Yes, we have checked that, don't worry."

"Ok then."

"Here is your itinerary. The flight is tomorrow. We will give you a hotel room to spend the night."

"Okay, thank you very much."

They handed me a flight itinerary. I checked the itinerary and told them that everything looked fine. One of the girls finished her duty for the day. She told me:

"Please follow me. I will help you to get a temporary visa stamp, bypass the security and get the taxi to reach the hotel."

"Oh, thank you very much." -I said and followed her.

Another of her colleagues joined us. As I was walking with the two girls on my two sides, being escorted like a VIP, I thought:

> This entire situation had plenty of potential to scare me. It was completely my fault that I did not check the transit visa requirements earlier. They could easily blame it on me and charge me for another ticket. The last moment ticket could have been prohibitively expensive and if I failed to pay, I could get stuck in Peru with an expired visa. But during this whole time I did not panic, I did not worry, I did not expect the worst to happen. On the contrary, I was so unusually calm that it could have aroused suspicion. I acted like it was a normal routine, as if I was expecting all of that to happen. That is very unlike me. Hmmm...something has happened...Yes, I know what it is. During these four months of travelling I have gone through so much uncertainty, so many setbacks and so many panic attacks. Some of the alarms were false alarms, some of the problems solved themselves and some of the situations demanded time and effort from me. But none of them could stop me, none of them harmed me and none of them killed me. Yes, I can feel it. It is evident. During this journey, something somewhere in me has changed. I am not the same as when I started.

A smile of contentment spontaneously appeared on my face. I knew that everything was going to be fine.

AFTERWORD

I hope you enjoyed reading this book. I need your help in order to make it available to as many people as possible so that they can benefit from my experiences or simply enjoy the stories.

You can help me by telling your family and friends about this book and writing a favorable review of the book on Amazon.com and other websites.

About the Author

Obaidur Rahaman, a native of India and a graduate of Indian Institute of Technology Bombay, obtained his PhD degree in computational chemistry from University of Delaware, USA. Obaidur lives in Weimar, Germany with his wife Darina and newborn baby Dimitar. When he is not in his office staring at the molecule on the computer screen, you might find him in the beautiful Ilm Park staring at the trees or at the fish in the river.

You can email him at obaidur.rahaman345@gmail.com
You can also follow him on facebook:
https://www.facebook.com/obaidur.rahaman.author/

A PREVIEW OF THE UPCOMING BOOK

The Night Hikers: A True Story Of Three Boy's Adventure, Survival And Friendship

By

Obaidur Rahaman

I was in a state between dead and alive. I lay down in the ditch by the side of the road and warm water flowed all over my body. I felt its warmth spreading all the way to the core of my heart. It caressed away my fatigue, it pacified my mind to a Zen-like state. I could finally give it a rest from constant thinking, planning and most of all worrying.

I raised my head to take a peek at the others. I saw Pondy lying down closeby, Machchhu was a bit farther away. We had no energy to talk. Tenzin and UD did not show any interest in getting in the water. They stood on the road and laughed at us. Tenzin kept making his typical silly jokes followed by hysterical guffaws. He never cared if anybody else found his jokes funny or not.

I was not in the mood of listening to his jokes. Instead I tried to remember what happened in the last two days. It all seemed like a bad dream.

A long time has passed since then. Fifteen years! In these fifteen years I have gone through the events of those two days many times in my mind. The memories are still there. When I try to recall them, they surface in my mind in a stream of fragmented pictures. Every time I go through them I alter them with my own imagination. Perhaps, by now, those memories diverged far away from reality. I wonder how my two companions Machchhu and Pondy think about those same events. I have listened to them telling some parts of the story to other people. I cannot say that I was satisfied with the way they narrated the story. Although, the facts were the same, their perspectives and descriptions were different from mine. I guess this is normal. Anyhow, I will tell you my version of the story, the only version I am capable of telling because for me that is the reality, my reality.

~ • ~

When I got admitted to Indian Institute of Technology Bombay (IITB) to earn my bachelor's degree, I had little idea about what was waiting for me there. Before arriving, I heard that the institute campus was surrounded by beautiful lakes and hills. There was a wildlife sanctuary close by. I also heard about the occasional visits of leopards and snakes to the campus. This was the first time I was going to live with a bunch of guys of my age without the constant surveillance of my parents. I was going to have the freedom to do whatever I wanted. I could hardly wait.

The last two years of painstaking preparation for the entrance examination burned me out. My craving for the unknown was channeled into the dreadful marshlands of integrals and differential equations. My power of imagination was used in visualizing intricate plays of electric and magnetic fields. My most adventurous days consisted of travelling in overcrowded buses to attend multiple private tuitions after the school hours. I was impatient to end my monotonous life in Kolkata and go somewhere faraway.

Both my parents accompanied me when I arrived at Mumbai. They helped me to settle down, made sure of everything and left after a couple of days. I bought a second-hand bicycle and started exploring the campus. My first glimpse of the Vihar lake from the hilltop was an overwhelming experience. The calm water of the abysmal lake reflected the mystic clouds hanging over it. A tiny island nebulously floated in the distance as if calling me to reveal a profound secret hidden in its chest. The lake was surrounded by green hills from all sides. It was as if a band of trolls came wandering through the forest, found the lake, quenched their thirst and fell asleep with their colossal bodies covered under lush green blankets. A spell of perpetual slumber was cast on them.

~ • ~

It was not until my second year that I went on my first trek. The idea of going on a trek came quite randomly. I was walking back to my hostel after a disastrous exam on a hot Friday afternoon, happy to be done with it and looking forward to the weekend. Right after passing through the hostel gate, I met Jagdeep Deogade, a shy and amiable guy who lived in the same hostel. He was loitering around the entrance after eating his afternoon snacks.

"What's up Jagdeep? You look bored," I said.

"Yeah buddy! All the local hostel residents are going home for the weekend. There is nothing much to do around here other than watching TV, reading books or playing computer games."

"Right, let's do something new dude."

"Yeah, that would be good. But do you have any ideas?"

"Hmmm...Let's go somewhere! Let's go on a trek! What do you say?"

"Excellent idea! It will be fun if we can make a group and go together."

"Yes! We can ask some people to join us."

"But it is too hot these days. I am not sure if people would be so enthusiastic about it."

"Let's go in the night then. It will be more fun, we will have a great adventure!"

"Do you think we can convince people to go in the night?"

"Maybe, I don't know. Let's ask Machchhu if he wants to join us!"

I was sure if there was only one person who would be

interested in such a whimsical, completely unplanned, last-moment idea, it was Machchhu. In fact, the stranger the idea was, the more irresistible it was for him. We used to call him *the josh machine* (the enthu machine) for his bottomless reserve of energy and impulsive activities. He delighted in the bizarre, adored the unpredictable and worshiped the impossible. Whenever somebody proposed a genuine and unconventional idea, it had an immense power over him. Like a malicious virus, it would creep up on his brain, take control over the gray matter, drive off any common sense and would not stop until it transformed into action, often resulting into disasters. Actually, he did not even need anybody to give him these ideas. He seemed to have access to these bizarre ideas from a hidden dimension where no commoner could barge in.

To give you an example, I can think of one rainy afternoon. It was raining really hard. Since I had no class at that time I stayed in the hostel. It got quite dark outside as if the evening arrived early that day. The gloomy sky and the monotonous noise of the raindrops made me feel very lazy. After eating our daily allowance of afternoon snacks, a few of us were looking for a warm and cozy place to start playing some card games when Machchhu came running from somewhere and said excitedly:

"It is raining like crazy! Let's climb up the *Mandir wala pahadi* (the hill with the temple)! Who wants to come with me?"

Everybody froze for a moment! The ones who did not know Machchhu very well struggled to trust their ears. Their faces clearly showed that they never heard anything more insane than that in their whole lives. The ones acquainted with Machchhu's whimsical nature whispered among themselves, "this is another of his diabolic plans" and "pretty soon you will see him in a hospital".

"Are you mad?" somebody yelled from the back.

A moment of silence followed and then everyone went back to minding their own business. Needless to say, Machchhu was habituated to such cold and apathetic responses. He did not lose hope and started pleading everybody. I felt sorry for him.

As a matter of fact I was attracted to Machchhu's proposal. To tell you the truth, it was irresistible for me. All my life, I could not even accidentally get wet by a drizzle without terribly worrying my mother and there was this chance to voluntarily go out in a heavy rain and climb up a hill! How could I say no to that?

It turned out that it was just me who agreed to accompany him. I dressed up quickly and took my umbrella. Machchhu told me:

"I have a good rain coat. Take my rain coat and I will take your umbrella."

I took up his offer and pretty soon we were outside walking toward the hill. We reached the base of the hill and started climbing it without wasting any time. I do not clearly remember how we managed to climb up that hill against the strong and erratic wind and water gushing down the muddy trail. Both the rain coat and the umbrella turned out to be absolutely useless. But we did not care. Pretty soon we found ourselves at the top, completely bedraggled. The positive side of that was that it took away all the worries about getting wet and we were ready to experience the thrill. From the top, we speechlessly watched the whole sky lashing on the hills all around us. We caught a glimpse of the tumultuous beauty of nature, something we miss every time we comfortably sit on a sofa watching TV on a rainy day. I would never do such a thing if it was not Machchhu who thought of it first.

So this was Machchhu.

He took over the plan of the night trek like it was his own. Interestingly we succeeded in finding four other people to join three of us on the trek.

We went to visit the fort of Rajamachi. Around midnight we arrived at the base of the hill and climbed up the gentle slope of the hill during the rest of the night taking short and long breaks in the middle. We made bonfire, played music, danced around the fire and took naps on the way. In the early morning we arrived at the top of the hill where the fort was built. We checked out the fort and started our journey back. On the way back we got into a little bit of trouble. But that is another story. The story I am going to tell you happened soon afterward.

Since we had a lot of fun and adventure on our first trek, we decided to go again two weeks later. That was perhaps too soon for another trek but I and Machchhu were very eager for more.

But unlike the last trip which went smoothly except the return journey, strange things started to happen to us this time. As we started to plan for the trek we felt as if a mysterious power was acting against it. We had little idea about what was waiting for us in that trip but from the beginning we got many signs that clearly told us not to go on this journey. I cannot think of another occasion when so many things went wrong one after another.

But these hindrances and misfortunes had the opposite effect on us. Instead of discouraging us they boosted our energy and strengthened our determination. The more it seemed to be impossible, the harder we tried. We constantly changed our plans to adapt to the new and adverse situations that arose on our path.

We made it happen. It had to happen.

When we proposed the plan for the second trek, all the seven people from the first trek showed interest. But we had a hunch that it was too good to be true.

In the afternoon of the planned day I met Machchhu just outside the gate of our hostel.

"Machchhu, I tried to talk to Jagdeep and Ashok but I could not find them. I guess they are not coming. How about your roommate Tenzin? Is he coming? And how about UD? They are coming right?" I asked him.

Machchhu was furious. "You can never trust these

guys. They always promise to come and don't say anything until the last moment when they come up with the lamest excuses in the world," he blurted out in disgust.

"So they are not coming?"

"Tenzin says that he has a loose motion and UD is not coming because he will have to finish his assignment," Machchhu said mockingly.

I got very disappointed hearing that. Since we felt that at least four or five people were needed for a trek in the night, canceling the trip seemed to be the only reasonable option under the circumstances. A day hike would be painful because of the heat and we wanted to have the fun and adventure of a night trek like the last one.

"How about Pondy? He seemed to be very enthusiastic last time I talked to him," I asked Machchhu.

"He is up for it and he has been really looking forward to it."

"Too bad that the other people dropped out."

"Yes, too bad. I hate these damn traitors."

We continued cursing the dropouts for a while. At the end, we realized that there was no use of getting mad at them. If they didn't want to go, they didn't want to go. There was nothing we could do about it. We could not force people to go on a hike, specially a night hike.

"You, me and Pondy," Machchhu finally said. "Three of us can still go, what do you think? We don't need these other people."

I thought for a moment and said "Why not? It will be like the last time, if we have done it once, we can do it again."

"And let's not go to Bhimashankar. Let's go to Harishchandragad, I heard that it is the most difficult trek around," Machchhu was boiling with enthusiasm.

"Hmmm..."

It sounded like a dangerous thing to do. I was a bit afraid of going to the most difficult trek, that also in the night. But then I thought we are probably not going to climb in the night but wait until daylight or something like that. As long as I had some company, I did not care much. So I agreed with him.

We ate our dinner, met up with Pondy and started.

As a preparation for the trek, we carried a couple of flashlights, about three liters of water, a radio, a roll of toilet paper, some bread and butter, a pack of cigarettes and a lighter, a towel and a bed cover to sit on. We did not have the time to think about anything else than the basic necessities. We first went to the store just outside the campus gate to buy some batteries for the flashlights. One of us came up with the idea of buying some lemons as a refreshment and remedy against the heat. We also bought a packet of salt to go with it. Since we did not have a knife to cut the lemons, we bought a blade that is normally used for shaving or cutting papers.

Little did we know how each of these items would be useful later.

We got into a train at Kanjurmarg station to reach Kalyan. I looked outside the window. The daylight was fading rapidly. The cool evening wind felt good on my face. The memories of the last trip were flashing in my mind. I remembered there was a full moon in the sky, exactly two weeks ago. But This time there was no moon at all.

Another sign of an inauspicious journey? May be.

What happens to the three boys on this fateful night hike? How do they get lost and how do they survive?

42525470R00103

Made in the USA
San Bernardino, CA
06 December 2016